THE MOVIE LOVER'S CHALLENGE

By Jamie Bowers

Alex – my movie partner in crime

Contents

Role Recall 1 1
Age Is Just a Number 1 2
Can You Reel The Love Tonight? 3
Roles on Roles 1 4
Keeping It Vague 1 5
Roles on Roles 2 6
Complete The Title 1 7
Familiar Phrases 1 8
Release Date Challenge 1 9
Movie Anagrams 1 10
Role Recall 2 11
Keeping It Vague 2 12
Age Is Just a Number 2 13
Complete The Title 2 14
Familiar Phrases 2 15
Release Date Challenge 2 16
Roles on Roles 3 17
Movie Anagrams 2 18
Role Recall 3 19
Keeping It Vague 3 20
Age Is Just a Number 3 21
Complete The Title 3 22
Familiar Phrases 3 23
Release Date Challenge 3 24
Movie Anagrams 3 25

Out of This World	26
Roles on Roles 4	27
Role Recall 4	28
Keeping It Vague 4	29
Age Is Just a Number 4	30
Complete The Title 4	31
Familiar Phrases 4	32
Release Date Challenge 4	33
Movie Anagrams 4	34
Role Recall 5	35
Keeping It Vague 5	36
Roles on Roles 5	37
Complete The Title 5	38
Age Is Just a Number 5	39
Familiar Phrases 5	40
Release Date Challenge 5	41
Movie Anagrams 5	42
Role Recall 6	43
Keeping It Vague 6	44
Age Is Just a Number 6	45
Roles on Roles 6	46
Complete The Title 6	47
Familiar Phrases 6	48
Release Date Challenge 6	49
Movie Anagrams 6	50
The Drama Diaries	51

Roles on Roles 7	52
Role Recall 7	53
Keeping It Vague 7	54
Complete The Title 7	55
Familiar Phrases 7	56
Release Date Challenge 7	57
Movie Anagrams 7	58
Lights, Camera, Laughter!	59
Same Name, Different Faces 1	60
Role Recall 8	61
Keeping It Vague 8	62
Roles on Roles 8	63
Complete The Title 8	64
Familiar Phrases 8	65
Release Date Challenge 8	66
Movie Anagrams 8	67
Role Recall 9	68
Dogs on Film	69
Keeping It Vague 9	70
Family Film Frenzy	71
Complete The Title 9	72
Familiar Phrases 9	73
Release Date Challenge 9	74
Movie Anagrams 9	75
Same Name, Different Faces 2	76
Role Recall 10	77

Keeping It Vague 10	78
Complete The Title 10	79
Roles on Roles 9	80
Familiar Phrases 10	81
Release Date Challenge 10	82
Movie Anagrams 10	83
Movie Villains	84
Roles on Roles 10	85
Famous Voices 1	86
Direct Orders 1	87
Famous Voices 2	87
Roles on Roles 11	89
Direct Orders 2	90
Blockbuster Brawls	90
Famous Voices 3	92
Direct Orders 3	93
Roles on Roles 12	93
Movie Taglines 1	95
Direct Orders 4	96
Movie Taglines 2	96
Direct Orders 5	98
Movie Taglines 3	98
Many Names, Same Face 1	100
Movie Taglines 4	101
Many Names, Same Face 2	102
Roles on Roles 13	103

Fright Night Flicks	104
Movie Taglines 5	105
Many Names, Same Face 3	106
Movie Taglines 6	107
The Real Name Game 1	108
Many Names, Same Face 4	109
Movie Taglines 7	110
Roles on Roles 14	111
The Real Name Game 2	112
True Stories	113
Many Names, Same Face 5	114
Movie Taglines 8	115
Many Names, Same Face 6	116
The Real Name Game 3	117
Movie Taglines 9	118
Many Names, Same Face 7	119
Roles on Roles 15	120
Movie Taglines 10	121
Many Names, Same Face 8	122
Fantasy Flicks	123
ANSWERS	**125**
Release Date Challenge 1 (Page 9)	128
Movie Anagrams 1 (Page 10)	129
Role Recall 2 (Page 11)	129
Keeping It Vague 2 (Page 12)	129
Age Is Just A Number 2 (Page 13)	130

Complete The Title 2 (Page 14)	130
Familiar Phrases 2 (Page 15)	131
Release Date Challenge 2 (Page 16)	131
Roles on Roles 3 (Page 17)	132
Movie Anagrams 2 (Page 18)	132
Role Recall 3 (Page 19)	132
Keeping It Vague 3 (Page 20)	132
Age Is Just A Number 3 (Page 21)	133
Complete The Title 3 (Page 22)	133
Familiar Phrases 3 (Page 23)	134
Movie Anagrams 3 (Page 25)	135
Out of This World (Page 26)	135
Roles on Roles 4 (Page 27)	135
Role Recall 4 (Page 28)	135
Keeping It Vague 4 (Page 29)	136
Age Is Just A Number 4 (Page 30)	136
Complete The Title 4 (Page 31)	137
Familiar Phrases 4 (Page 32)	137
Release Date Challenge 4 (Page 33)	137
Movie Anagrams 4 (Page 34)	138
Role Recall 5 (Page 35)	138
Keeping It Vague 5 (Page 36)	139
Roles on Roles 5 (Page 37)	139
Complete The Title 5 (Page 38)	139
Age Is Just A Number 5 (Page 39)	139
Familiar Phrases 5 (Page 40)	140

Release Date Challenge 5 (Page 41)	140
Movie Anagrams 5 (Page 42)	141
Role Recall 6 (Page 43)	141
Keeping It Vague 6 (Page 44)	142
Age Is Just A Number 6 (Page 45)	142
Roles on Roles 6 (Page 46)	142
Complete The Title 6 (Page 47)	143
Familiar Phrases 6 (Page 48)	143
Release Date Challenge 6 (Page 49)	143
Movie Anagrams 6 (Page 50)	144
The Drama Diaries (Page 51)	144
Roles on Roles 7 (Page 52)	145
Role Recall 7 (Page 53)	145
Keeping It Vague 7 (Page 54)	145
Complete The Title 7 (Page 55)	145
Familiar Phrases 7 (Page 56)	146
Release Date Challenge 7 (Page 57)	146
Movie Anagrams 7 (Page 58)	147
Lights, Camera, Laughter! (Page 59)	147
Same Name, Different Faces 1 (Page 60)	147
Role Recall 8 (Page 61)	148
Keeping It Vague 8 (Page 62)	148
Roles on Roles 8 (Page 63)	148
Complete The Title 8 (Page 64)	148
Familiar Phrases 8 (Page 65)	149
Release Date Challenge 8 (Page 66)	149

Movie Anagrams 8 (Page 67) 150

Role Recall 9 (Page 68) 150

Dogs on Film (Page 69) 150

Keeping It Vague 9 (Page 70) 151

Family Film Frenzy (Page 71) 151

Complete The Title 9 (Page 72) 151

Familiar Phrases 9 (Page 73) 152

Release Date Challenge 9 (Page 74) 152

Movie Anagrams 9 (Page 75) 153

Same Name, Different Faces 2 (Page 76) 153

Role Recall 10 (Page 77) 153

Keeping It Vague 10 (Page 78) 154

Complete The Title 10 (Page 79) 154

Roles on Roles 9 (Page 80) 154

Familiar Phrases 10 (Page 81) 154

Release Date Challenge 10 (Page 82) 155

Movie Anagrams 10 (Page 83) 155

Movie Villains (Page 84) 156

Roles on Roles 10 (Page 85) 156

Famous Voices 1 (Page 86) 156

Direct Orders 1 (Page 87) 157

Famous Voices 2 (Page 88) 157

Roles on Roles 11 (Page 89) 158

Direct Orders 2 (Page 90) 158

Blockbuster Brawls (Page 91) 159

Famous Voices 3 (Page 92) 159

Direct Orders 3 (Page 93) 159
Roles on Roles 12 (Page 94) 160
Movie Taglines 1 (Page 95) 160
Direct Orders 4 (Page 96) 161
Movie Taglines 2 (Page 97) 162
Direct Orders 5 (Page 98) 162
Movie Taglines 3 (Page 99) 163
Many Names, Same Face 1 (Page 100) 163
Movie Taglines 4 (Page 101) 163
Many Names, Same Face 2 (Page 102) 164
Roles on Roles 13 (Page 103) 164
Fright Night Flicks (Page 104) 164
Movie Taglines 5 (Page 105) 164
Many Names, Same Face 3 (Page 106) 165
Movie Taglines 6 (Page 107) 165
The Real Name Game 1 (Page 108) 165
Many Names, Same Face 4 (Page 109) 166
Movie Taglines 7 (Page 110) 166
Roles on Roles 14 (Page 111) 166
The Real Name Game 2 (Page 112) 167
True Stories (Page 113) 167
Many Names, Same Face 5 (Page 114) 167
Movie Taglines 8 (Page 115) 168
Many Names, Same Face 6 (Page 116) 168
The Real Name Game 3 (Page 117) 168
Movie Taglines 9 (Page 118) 168

Many Names, Same Face 7 (Page 119) 169

Roles on Roles 15 (Page 120) 169

Movie Taglines 10 (Page 121) 169

Many Names, Same Face 8 (Page 122) 170

Fantasy Flicks (Page 123) 170

INTRODUCTION

Step into the dazzling world of cinema, where every frame tells a story and every scene holds a secret. Whether you're a casual moviegoer or a dedicated cinephile, this comprehensive collection of movie trivia will test your knowledge across decades of filmmaking magic.

From the golden age of Hollywood to contemporary blockbusters, this quiz book takes you on an exciting journey through the silver screen's most memorable moments.
Whether you're hosting a movie night, preparing for pub trivia, or simply wanting to challenge yourself, this collection offers varying difficulty levels to engage both newcomers and seasoned film buffs alike.

So, dim the lights, grab your popcorn, and prepare to put your movie knowledge to the ultimate test. The projector is rolling, and your adventure through cinema history begins now.
Lights, camera, action!

THE MOVIE LOVER'S CHALLENGE

Role Recall 1

Is it possible for you to name the actor and film by using the name of the character and the year in which the movie was released?

1. Tyler Durden (1999)

2. Patrick Bateman (2000)

3. Dominic Toretto (2001)

4. Tony Montana (1983)

5. Annie Wilkes (1990)

6. Scar (1994)

7. Jack Dawson (1997)

8. William Wallace (1995)

9. Ego (2017)

10. Bullet-Tooth Tony (2000)

THE MOVIE LOVER'S CHALLENGE

Age Is Just a Number 1

Put these actors in order they were born, starting with the earliest.

1. Tom Hanks
   Meryl Streep
   Leonardo DiCaprio
   Julia Roberts
   Brad Pitt

2. Sandra Bullock
   Denzel Washington
   Cate Blanchett
   Johnny Depp
   Dwayne Johnson

3. Robert De Niro
   Angelina Jolie
   Will Smith
   Nicole Kidman
   Morgan Freeman

THE MOVIE LOVER'S CHALLENGE

Can You Reel The Love Tonight?

1. In the movie "The Notebook," what is the name of the male lead character played by Ryan Gosling?
2. What is the 1990 romantic movie featuring Patrick Swayze and Demi Moore with a supernatural connection?
3. Which romantic movie is based on the Jane Austen novel and follows the story of Elizabeth and Mr. Darcy?
4. In the film "Titanic," what is the name of the necklace that Bill Paxton's character is searching for?
5. Which romantic comedy follows the story of a man who can hear women's thoughts after a magical encounter?
6. In the movie "500 Days of Summer," what is the name of the character played by Joseph Gordon-Levitt?
7. Which romantic comedy stars Sandra Bullock as Margaret Tate, a Canadian executive facing deportation from the United States?
8. During their initial meeting in the movie "Serendipity", what do Jonathan and Sara agree not to exchange?
9. The romantic film "Her" features the voice of an AI operating system. Who voiced the AI character?
10. In the film "La La Land," what city does Mia Dolan pursue her dreams in?

THE MOVIE LOVER'S CHALLENGE

Roles on Roles 1

Can you name the actor who has appeared in each set of movies?

1. The Hurt Locker
   Wind River
   The Town
   Avengers Assemble

2. The Hunger Games
   The Lego Movie
   Pitch Perfect
   Power Rangers

3. The Dark Knight
   Thank You For Smoking
   The Core
   Rabbit Hole

4. The House Bunny
   Just Friends
   Scary Movie
   The Emoji Movie

5. Chicago
   Guardians of the Galaxy
   Boogie Nights
   Step Brothers

THE MOVIE LOVER'S CHALLENGE

Keeping It Vague 1

Can you guess the movie based on a vague description?

1. A young FBI trainee seeks the insights of a brilliant but incarcerated criminal to apprehend a gruesome serial killer on the loose. As they navigate a complex psychological game, the trainee must confront her own fears and delve into the darkest corners of the human psyche to solve the case. (1991)

2. In a bustling desert city, a charismatic street-smart individual discovers a mystical lamp containing a wish-granting power, leading them on a thrilling journey to navigate palace intrigues, unmask hidden identities, and ultimately alter their destiny. With the lamp's magic, they must confront an ambitious sorcerer and win the heart of a spirited and resourceful companion to triumph against all odds. (1992)

3. A group of illusionists with exceptional skills in magic and misdirection team up to pull off a series of elaborate heists during their mesmerizing live performances, all while evading a determined law enforcement agent hot on their trail. As their daring feats captivate the world, a hidden agenda begins to unravel, leading to a mind-bending revelation that blurs the line between illusion and reality. (2013)

THE MOVIE LOVER'S CHALLENGE

Roles on Roles 2

Can you name the actor who has appeared in each set of movies?

1. Into the Wild
   Speed Racer
   The Girl Next Door
   The Darkest Hour

2. 13 Going on 30
   Jurassic World
   Ant-Man
   27 resses

3. Les Misérables
   Dear John
   Mean Girls
   Letters to Juliet

4. American Hustle
   Crash
   End of Watch
   Ant-Man

5. Casper
   Buffalo '66
   Speed Racer
   After Life

THE MOVIE LOVER'S CHALLENGE

Complete The Title 1

Challenge yourself to fill in the missing word from these movie titles.

1. The Shape of _____ (2006, Sally Hawkins)

2. The _____ of Everything (2014, Eddie Redmayne)

3. Monty _____ and the Holy Grail (1975, Graham Chapman)

4. _____ Animals (2016, Amy Adams)

5. Crouching Tiger, _____ Dragon (2000, Chow Yun-Fat)

6. _____ Fiction (1994, John Travolta)

7. Crazy _____ Asians (2018, Constance Wu)

8. Green _____ (2018, Viggo Mortensen)

9. _____ Fair Lady (1964, Audrey Hepburn)

10. Gone _____ the Wind (1939, Clark Gable)

THE MOVIE LOVER'S CHALLENGE

Familiar Phrases 1

Can you identify the movie that first made these iconic quotes famous?

1. May the Force be with you. (1977)

2. Here's looking at you, kid. (1942)

3. I'll be back. (1984)

4. Why so serious? (2008)

5. You can't handle the truth! (1992)

6. There's no place like home. (1939)

7. I'm king of the world! (1997)

8. I'll have what she's having. (1989)

9. I see dead people. (1999)

10. Life is like a box of chocolates; you never know what you're gonna get. (1994)

THE MOVIE LOVER'S CHALLENGE

Release Date Challenge 1

Put these movies in order of their initial cinema release, starting with the oldest one.

1. The Silence of the Lambs
   Pulp Fiction
   Schindler's List
   Titanic
   Goodfellas

2. Jurassic Park
   The Shawshank Redemption
   Terminator 2: Judgment Day
   The Matrix
   Saving Private Ryan

3. Forrest Gump
   Fight Club
   Fargo
   Braveheart
   Home Alone

THE MOVIE LOVER'S CHALLENGE

Movie Anagrams 1

Unscramble the letters to reveal the movie title.

1. chopsy (1960 - Horror/ Thriller)

2. in attic (1997 - Romance/ Drama)

3. corky (1976 - Drama/ Sport)

4. forged the hat (1972 - Crime/ Drama)

5. not cup if lip (1994 - Crime/ Drama)

6. hi deer known has the stamp (1994 - Crime/ Drama)

7. the balls mince the foes (1991 - Thriller/ Horror)

8. keg darth think (2008 - Action/ Adventure)

9. cop in nite (2010 - Action/ Sci-fi)

10. tell strainer (2014 - Sci-fi/ Adventure)

THE MOVIE LOVER'S CHALLENGE

Role Recall 2

Is it possible for you to name the actor and film by using the name of the character and the year in which the movie was released?

1. Martin Blank (1997)

2. Holly Golightly (1961)

3. Miranda Priestly (2006)

4. Lloyd Christmas (1994)

5. Dr Ian Malcolm (1993)

6. Lester Burnham (1999)

7. Walt Disney (2013)

8. Danny Zuko (1978)

9. Sarah Connor (1984)

10. Carl Denham (2005)

THE MOVIE LOVER'S CHALLENGE

Keeping It Vague 2

Can you guess the movie based on a vague description?

1. In a world controlled by a powerful and mysterious system, a group of rebels discovers the truth about their reality and launches a daring mission to awaken humanity from its manipulated existence, leading to a battle between perception and truth that blurs the line between the digital and physical realms. (1999)

2. In a remote island wildlife sanctuary, an ambitious venture to resurrect prehistoric creatures through advanced genetic engineering turns into a perilous struggle for survival when the manufactured creatures break free from their enclosures, forcing a group of people to navigate the treacherous landscape to escape. (1993)

3. A young boy forms an unexpected and heartwarming connection with a stranded visitor from another world, leading him on an adventure to help the visitor return home while evading government agents who are determined to capture the mysterious being. As their bond deepens, the boy and the visitor discover the power of friendship and the importance of understanding across worlds. (1982)

THE MOVIE LOVER'S CHALLENGE

Age Is Just a Number 2

Put these actors in order they were born, starting with the earliest.

1. Kate Winslet
   George Clooney
   Natalie Portman
   Matt Damon
   Tom Hardy

2. Harrison Ford
   Christian Slater
   Samuel L. Jackson
   Benedict Cumberbatch
   Al Pacino

3. Dustin Hoffman
   Sean Connery
   Emma Watson
   Liam Neeson
   Jennifer Aniston

THE MOVIE LOVER'S CHALLENGE

Complete The Title 2

Challenge yourself to fill in the missing word from these movie titles.

1. 12 Angry _____ (1957, Henry Fonda)

2. The _____ Horse Thieves (1976, Alastair Sim)

3. _____ and the Beast (2017, Emma Watson)

4. Peter _____ (1953, Bobby Driscoll)

5. A _____ Place (2018, Emily Blunt)

6. The Hobbit: The _____ of Smaug (2013, Martin Freeman)

7. Fantastic Beasts and Where to _____ Them (2016, Eddie Redmayne)

8. A _____ Mind (2001, Russell Crowe)

9. The _____ Book (2016, Bill Murray)

10. Hell or _____ Water (2016, Chris Pine)

THE MOVIE LOVER'S CHALLENGE

Familiar Phrases 2

Can you identify the movie that first made these iconic quotes famous?

1. I'm just a girl, standing in front of a boy, asking him to love her. (1999)

2. Here's Johnny! (1980)

3. You talking to me? (1976)

4. Keep your friends close, but your enemies closer. (1974)

5. I feel the need... the need for speed! (1986)

6. You can't buy happiness, but you can buy a bicycle, and that's pretty close. (1985)

7. Houston, we have a problem. (1995)

8. I need to know that it's possible that two people can stay happy together forever. (2007)

9. Bond. James Bond. (1962)

10. Say hello to my little friend! (1983)

THE MOVIE LOVER'S CHALLENGE

Release Date Challenge 2

Put these movies in order of their initial cinema release, starting with the oldest one.

1. The Sixth Sense
   Independence Day
   Speed
   Men in Black
   The Truman Show

2. Dumb and Dumber
   A Few Good Men
   The Dark Knight
   Avatar
   The Lord of the Rings: The Fellowship of the Ring

3. Inception
   Gladiator
   The Bourne Identity
   Finding Nemo
   The Departed

THE MOVIE LOVER'S CHALLENGE

Roles on Roles 3

Can you name the actor who has appeared in each set of movies?

1. Election
   We Were Soldiers
   Just Friends
   American Pie

2. The Duff
   One Fine Day
   Hope Floats
   The Perks of Being a Wallflower

3. There Will Be Blood
   Prisoners
   Little Miss Sunshine
   12 Years a Slave

4. Gone Girl
   Die Another Day
   Pride & Prejudice
   Jack Reacher

5. The Killing
   RoboCop
   Suicide Squad
   The Secrets We Keep

THE MOVIE LOVER'S CHALLENGE

Movie Anagrams 2

Unscramble the letters to reveal the movie title.

1. strum for peg (1994 - Drama/ Romance)

2. nil childs rests (1993 - War/ Drama)

3. gale floods (1990 - Crime/ Drama)

4. tax mither (1999 - Action/ Sci-fi)

5. tire green hen (1999 - Drama/ Crime)

6. hex store tic (1973 - Horror/ Thriller)

7. keen as yes (1998 - Thriller/ Crime)

8. no pay owe scalp (1979 - War/ Drama)

9. leons wet cone fever cooks hut (1975 - Drama/ Comedy)

10. connect fern hitch one (1971 - Drama/ Crime)

THE MOVIE LOVER'S CHALLENGE

Role Recall 3

Is it possible for you to name the actor and film by using the name of the character and the year in which the movie was released?

1. Clarice Starling (1991)

2. Mrs Robinson (1967)

3. Tommy DeVito (1990)

4. Red (1994)

5. Harry Callahan (1971)

6. Dr Hannibal Lecter (1991)

7. John Connor (1991)

8. Bubba Blue (1994)

9. Mark Zuckerberg (2010)

10. The Bride (2003)

THE MOVIE LOVER'S CHALLENGE

Keeping It Vague 3

Can you guess the movie based on a vague description?

1. A brilliant college student's ambition to connect people through a revolutionary online platform leads him down a tumultuous path of friendships, betrayals, and legal battles, as his creation transforms into a global phenomenon with unforeseen consequences. The movie explores the rise and fall of a digital empire, unveiling the complex interplay of innovation, ambition, and personal conflicts. (2010)

2. In a whimsical and ornate European hotel, a dedicated concierge becomes entangled in a web of mystery and intrigue when he inherits a valuable piece of art, setting off a chain of events that lead to unexpected alliances and comedic escapades across picturesque landscapes. As the chase unfolds, the characters navigate eccentric personalities, hidden secrets, and a race against time to solve the puzzle and safeguard their futures. (2014)

3. In a bustling city known for its artistic pulse, two ambitious individuals from different creative spheres cross paths and navigate the delicate balance between their dreams and the realities of love and career. Their passionate pursuit of success challenges their connection, leading them through a mesmerizing dance of highs and lows in the vibrant backdrop of the entertainment industry. (2016)

THE MOVIE LOVER'S CHALLENGE

Age Is Just a Number 3

Put these actors in order they were born, starting with the earliest.

1. Daniel Day-Lewis
   Gwyneth Paltrow
   Russell Crowe
   Penelope Cruz
   Tom Cruise

2. Keira Knightley
   Robert Downey Jr
   Halle Berry
   Hugh Jackman
   Kate Hudson

3. Jack Nicholson
   Cameron Diaz
   Clint Eastwood
   Amy Adams
   Jamie Foxx

THE MOVIE LOVER'S CHALLENGE

Complete The Title 3

Challenge yourself to fill in the missing word from these movie titles.

1. The _____ Eight (2015, Samuel L Jackson)

2. The Sound of _____ (1965, Julie Andrews)

3. _____ Dogs (1992, Harvey Keitel)

4. _____ Kingdom (2012, Jared Gilman)

5. The _____ Network (2010, Jesse Eisenberg)

6. The Grand _____ Hotel (2014, Ralph Fiennes)

7. The _____ of Wall Street (2013, Leonardo DiCaprio)

8. The Sixth _____ (1999, Bruce Willis)

9. Alice in _____ (2010, Mia Wasikowska)

10. Inside _____ (2015, Amy Poehler)

THE MOVIE LOVER'S CHALLENGE

Familiar Phrases 3

Can you identify the movie that first made these iconic quotes famous?

1. Hasta la vista, baby. (1991)

2. To infinity and beyond! (1995)

3. Why, hello, Clarice. (1991)

4. I love the smell of napalm in the morning. (1979)

5. I'm just one stomach flu away from my goal weight. (2006)

6. There's no crying in baseball! (1992)

7. Show me the money! (1996)

8. I am your father. (1980)

9. I'm walking here! (1969)

10. You had me at hello. (1996)

THE MOVIE LOVER'S CHALLENGE

Release Date Challenge 3

Put these movies in order of their initial cinema release, starting with the oldest one.

1. Spider-Man
   Memento
   Pirates of the Caribbean: The Curse of the Black Pearl
   The Notebook
   The Hangover

2. Star Wars: Episode IV - A New Hope
   The Godfather
   Raiders of the Lost Ark
   Rocky
   Blade Runner

3. Jaws
   Die Hard
   The Terminator
   Dirty Dancing
   Back to the Future

THE MOVIE LOVER'S CHALLENGE

Movie Anagrams 3

Unscramble the letters to reveal the movie title.

1. tweak riding hover beer hit (1957 - War/ Drama)

2. giver to (1958 - Mystery/ Thriller)

3. a thug ate red (1967 - Romance/ Drama)

4. a mud sea (1984 - Drama/ Musical)

5. zit cake nine (1941 - Drama/ Mystey)

6. a clan a scab (1942 - Romance/ Drama)

7. whined to the wing (1939 - Romance/ Drama)

8. in angries in thin (1952 - Musical/ Romance)

9. shoot lime kite (1959 - Comedy/ Romance)

10. wear lie an orca fab (1962 - War/ Drama)

THE MOVIE LOVER'S CHALLENGE

Out of This World

1. In the movie "Blade Runner," what is the term used for the human-like androids that are indistinguishable from humans?
2. What is the name of the virtual reality world in the movie "Ready Player One"?
3. Who directed the 1977 sci-fi film "Close Encounters of the Third Kind"?
4. Who plays the role of Morpheus in the 1999 movie "The Matrix"?
5. In "Back to the Future", what speed does the DeLorean need to reach in order for it to travel through time?
6. Which sci-fi comedy first introduced us to a group of intergalactic misfits led by Peter Quill?
7. In the film "Interstellar," what is the name of the spaceship that carries the astronauts on their mission through the wormhole?
8. What is the name of the alien species in the movie "Avatar"?
9. Who plays the character of Katniss Everdeen in "The Hunger Games" film series?
10. In the movie "Pacific Rim," what are the giant humanoid robots called, which are controlled by two pilots?

THE MOVIE LOVER'S CHALLENGE

Roles on Roles 4

Can you name the actor who has appeared in each set of movies?

1. Adaptation
   Troy
   Zodiac
   X-Men 2

2. Inception
   Looper
   Don Jon
   50/50

3. The Hunger Games: Catching Fire
   Contact
   The Neon Demon
   Consecration

4. Training Day
   Before Sunrise
   Valerian and the City of a Thousand Planets
   The Purge

5. Three Billboards Outside Ebbing, Missouri
   Seven Psychopaths
   Geostorm
   Limitless

THE MOVIE LOVER'S CHALLENGE

Role Recall 4

Is it possible for you to name the actor and film by using the name of the character and the year in which the movie was released?

1. Steven Kovacs (1996)

2. Marty McFly (1985)

3. Axel Foley (1984)

4. Dr Peter Venkman (1984)

5. The Dude (1998)

6. Buck Russell (1989)

7. Morpheus (1999)

8. Arthur Fleck (2019)

9. Ellen Ripley (1979)

10. Tonto (2013)

THE MOVIE LOVER'S CHALLENGE

Keeping It Vague 4

Can you guess the movie based on a vague description?

1. In a lush and mysterious alien world, a human explorer becomes entangled in the conflict between an indigenous population and a powerful corporate entity, as he discovers his loyalties shifting and the true nature of the world he thought he understood. With themes of cultural clash and environmentalism, the explorer must navigate moral complexities and forge unexpected alliances to protect the planet's delicate balance. (2009)

2. A coastal town is terrorized by a relentless and unseen oceanic threat, forcing a group of individuals to venture into dangerous waters to confront the menace and protect their community. As tension mounts, they must navigate personal conflicts while facing a formidable adversary lurking beneath the waves. (1975)

3. In a modern metropolis, a disillusioned office worker forms an underground group that challenges societal norms through acts of rebellion, sparking an unconventional movement. As the group's activities escalate, the line between reality and illusion blurs, leading to a mind-bending exploration of identity and conformity. (1999)

THE MOVIE LOVER'S CHALLENGE

Age Is Just a Number 4

Put these actors in order they were born, starting with the earliest.

1. Reese Witherspoon
   Ryan Gosling
   Jodie Foster
   Mark Wahlberg
   Julianne Moore

2. Colin Firth
   Charlize Theron
   Michael Fassbender
   Anne Hathaway
   Eddie Murphy

3. Marion Cotillard
   Matthew McConaughey
   Jennifer Lawrence
   Christian Bale
   Rachel McAdams

THE MOVIE LOVER'S CHALLENGE

Complete The Title 4

Challenge yourself to fill in the missing word from these movie titles.

1. _____ One: A Star Wars Story (2016, Felicity Jones)

2. The Green _____ (1999, Tom Hanks)

3. Lady and the _____ (1955, Barbara Luddy)

4. Blue is the _____ Color (2013, Lea Seydoux)

5. The Ballad of Buster _____ (2018, Tim Blake Nelson)

6. _____ Unchained (2012, Jamie Foxx)

7. The _____ Show (1998, Jim Carrey)

8. The _____ Stallion (1979, Mickey Rooney)

9. American _____ (1999, Kevin Spacey)

10. _____ Story (2019, Adam Driver)

THE MOVIE LOVER'S CHALLENGE

Familiar Phrases 4

Can you identify the movie that first made these iconic quotes famous?

1. I'm not bad. I'm just drawn that way. (1988)

2. You shall not pass! (2001)

3. I drink your milkshake! (2007)

4. I'm not a smart man, but I know what love is. (1994)

5. I'm the Dude. So that's what you call me. (1998)

6. I'm just a kid from Brooklyn. (2011)

7. He can't see without his glasses!! (1991)

8. I'm the king of the world! (1997)

9. Yippie-ki-yay! (1988)

10. I'm gonna make him an offer he can't refuse. (1972)

THE MOVIE LOVER'S CHALLENGE

Release Date Challenge 4

Put these movies in order of their initial cinema release, starting with the oldest one.

1. Casablanca
   The Sound of Music
   La La Land
   The Exorcist
   The Social Network

2. Black Panther
   The Dark Knight Rises
   The Grand Budapest Hotel
   The King's Speech
   The Shape of Water

3. Easy Rider
   The Graduate
   The French Connection
   The Sting
   One Flew Over the Cuckoo's Nest

THE MOVIE LOVER'S CHALLENGE

Movie Anagrams 4

Unscramble the letters to reveal the movie title.

1. come fund his outs (1965 - Musical/ Romance)

2. no mighty cow bid (1969 - Drama/ Buddy)

3. ok croc a wrong lake (1971 - Drama/ Crime)

4. fat dye rad go noon (1975 - Crime/ Drama)

5. rent wok (1976 - Drama/ Comedy)

6. ah nil lane (1977 - Romance/ Comedy)

7. i ram nan (1988 - Drama/ Road)

8. gin hull wood ting (1997 - Drama/ Romance)

9. I meaty braun ace (1999 - Romance/ Drama)

10. grail toad (2000 - Action/ Adventure)

THE MOVIE LOVER'S CHALLENGE

Role Recall 5

Is it possible for you to name the actor and film by using the name of the character and the year in which the movie was released?

1. George Banks (1991)

2. Alonzo Harris (2001)

3. Dr Frank-N-Furter (1975)

4. Dewey Finn (2003)

5. Malcolm Crowe (1999)

6. Gale Weathers (1996)

7. Cobb (2010)

8. Jules Winnfield (1994)

9. Mr Pink (1992)

10. Carrie Bradshaw (2008)

THE MOVIE LOVER'S CHALLENGE

Keeping It Vague 5

Can you guess the movie based on a vague description?

1. Infiltrating a tight-knit group of adrenaline-seeking individuals, a determined law enforcement officer goes undercover to expose a string of daring heists connected to extreme sports, leading to a perilous clash of loyalties as he becomes entangled in their dangerous world. As bonds form and risks escalate, the line between right and wrong blurs, forcing the officer to question his mission and allegiances. (1991)

2. An eccentric scientist's time-traveling invention inadvertently sends a high school student decades into the past. Desperate to return to his own time, he must ensure his parents' romance while navigating the challenges of altering the course of history. (1985)

3. In a gritty urban setting, an underdog fighter with dreams of greatness embraces an unexpected opportunity for a shot at the championship, pushing his physical and emotional limits to prove his worth and inspire those around him. Through intense training and unyielding determination, he navigates a turbulent journey of self-discovery and redemption. (1976)

THE MOVIE LOVER'S CHALLENGE

Roles on Roles 5

Can you name the actor who has appeared in each set of movies?

1. This Is The End -- The Sorcerer's Apprentice -- Night at the Museum 2 -- How To Train Your Dragon

2. 300 -- Dredd -- Pride and Prejudice and Zombies -- Fighting with My Family

3. The Perks of Being a Wallflower -- Anchorman 2: The Legend Continues -- I Love You, Man -- Avengers: Endgame

4. The Happening -- Trolls -- 500 Days of Summer -- Elf

5. Crash -- Gosford Park -- 54 -- Cruel Intentions

THE MOVIE LOVER'S CHALLENGE

Complete The Title 5

Challenge yourself to fill in the missing word from these movie titles.

1. _____ Now (1979, Martin Sheen)

2. _____ Ridge (2016, Andrew Garfield)

3. _____ Out (2019, Daniel Craig)

4. The _____ Short (2015, Christian Bale)

5. Lost _____ Translation (2003, Bill Murray)

6. Full _____ Jacket (1987, Matthew Modine)

7. The Great _____ (1963, Steve McQueen)

8. The Bridge on the River _____ (1957, Alec Guinness)

9. _____ Driver (2017, Ansel Elgort)

10. _____ & Company (1988, Joey Lawrence)

THE MOVIE LOVER'S CHALLENGE

Age Is Just a Number 5

Put these actors in order they were born, starting with the earliest.

1. Eddie Redmayne
   Michelle Pfeiffer
   Ben Affleck
   Brie Larson
   Ryan Reynolds

2. Viola Davis
   Chris Pratt
   Octavia Spencer
   Chadwick Boseman
   Margot Robbie

3. Mahershala Ali
   Gal Gadot
   Lupita Nyong'o
   Jason Momoa
   Emma Stone

THE MOVIE LOVER'S CHALLENGE

Familiar Phrases 5

Can you identify the movie that first made these iconic quotes famous?

1. Wax on, wax off. (1984)

2. Nobody's perfect. (1959)

3. Beneath this mask, there is more than just flesh, Mr. Creedy. Beneath this mask, there is an idea. And ideas are bulletproof. (2006)

4. Roads, where we're going we don't need roads. (1996)

5. I'm your Huckleberry. (1993)

6. I am serious. And don't call me Shirley. (1979)

7. You know it's all funny until somebody gets shot in the leg. (1998)

8. He doesn't have a name so Death can't find him! (1995)

9. Let's kick the tires and
 light the fires, big daddy! (1996)

10. I need a corporal. You're it, until you're dead or I find someone better. (1997)

THE MOVIE LOVER'S CHALLENGE

Release Date Challenge 5

Put these movies in order of their initial cinema release, starting with the oldest one.

1. A Clockwork Orange
   Alien
   The Rocky Horror Picture Show
   Close Encounters of the Third Kind
   Taxi Driver

2. Lost in Translation
   Spirited Away
   No Country for Old Men
   Up
   The Aviator

3. Black Swan
   Mad Max: Fury Road
   Get Out
   Arrival
   The Hurt Locker

THE MOVIE LOVER'S CHALLENGE

Movie Anagrams 5

Unscramble the letters to reveal the movie title.

1. sun tom the bean layer (2001 - Comedy/ Drama)

2. snots not in a lil rat (2003 - Romance/ Drama)

3. crow stain hot leek (2010 - Drama/ Historical Drama)

4. gut toe (2017 - Horror/ Thriller)

5. a step air (2019 - Thriller/ Drama)

6. clone the false mat (1941 - Noir/ Crime)

7. model unity in bed (1944 - Noir/ Crime)

8. not wet hear front (1954 - Drama/ Romance)

9. out ale brace with sue (1955 - Drama/ Romance)

10. fantasy freaks fit bat (1961 - Romance/ Comedy)

THE MOVIE LOVER'S CHALLENGE

Role Recall 6

Is it possible for you to name the actor and film by using the name of the character and the year in which the movie was released?

1. Will Scarlet (1991)

2. Captain John Miller (1998)

3. Alfred Pennyworth (2005)

4. Marge Gunderson (1996)

5. Derek Vinyard (1998)

6. Tony Stark (2008)

7. Vincent Benedict (1988)

8. Travis Bickle (1976)

9. John McClane (1988)

10. Sally Albright (1989)

THE MOVIE LOVER'S CHALLENGE

Keeping It Vague 6

Can you guess the movie based on a vague description?

1. A desperate mother seeks the help of a determined spiritual expert when her daughter becomes inexplicably plagued by sinister and otherworldly forces, leading to a harrowing battle against an ancient evil that tests the limits of faith and sanity. As the struggle intensifies, the line between reality and the supernatural blurs, threatening to consume them both. (1973)

2. In a dystopian future, a young man with a penchant for violence becomes the subject of an experimental rehabilitation program that aims to suppress his aggressive tendencies, raising questions about free will, morality, and the limits of societal control. As his behavior is altered, he grapples with a newfound internal struggle that challenges both his nature and the society's methods. (1971)

3. A group of friends from a tight-knit industrial town are profoundly impacted by their experiences during the Vietnam War, leading to their struggle to find meaning and solace amidst the emotional scars of their shared past. The story delves into their bond and resilience as they navigate post-war life, reflecting on the enduring effects of trauma and the search for hope. (1978)

THE MOVIE LOVER'S CHALLENGE

Age Is Just a Number 6

Put these actors in order they were born, starting with the earliest.

1. Idris Elba
   Sylvester Stallone
   Arnold Schwarzenegger
   Tessa Thompson
   Joaquin Phoenix

2. Mel Gibson
   Rami Malek
   Carey Elwes
   Adam Driver
   Florence Pugh

3. Chris Hemsworth
   Chris Evans
   Oscar Isaac
   Neve Campbell
   John Boyega

THE MOVIE LOVER'S CHALLENGE

Roles on Roles 6

Can you name the actor who has appeared in each set of movies?

1. The Last Kiss
   The To-Do List
   Life Happens
   Jumper

2. Hairspray
   Enchanted
   X-Men
   27 Dresses

3. Just Married
   Girl, Interrupted
   8 Mile
   Clueless

4. Inception
   Sunshine
   The Dark Knight
   28 Days Later

5. Surrogates
   Cop Out
   Glass
   The Fifth Element

THE MOVIE LOVER'S CHALLENGE

Complete The Title 6

Challenge yourself to fill in the missing word from these movie titles.

1. _____ of Dogs (2018, Bryan Cranston)

2. A _____ Orange (1971, Malcolm McDowell)

3. Lawrence of _____ (1962, Peter O'Toole)

4. The King's _____ (2010, Colin Firth)

5. _____ Basterds (2009, Brad Pitt)

6. The Day the Earth Stood _____ (2008, Keanu Reeves)

7. Doctor _____ (2016, Benedict Cumberbatch)

8. _____ Reformed (2017, Ethan Hawke)

9. Black _____ (2018, Chadwick Boseman)

10. Once Upon a Time in _____ (2019, Leonardo DiCaprio)

THE MOVIE LOVER'S CHALLENGE

Familiar Phrases 6

Can you identify the movie that first made these iconic quotes famous?

1. Serve the public trust, protect the innocent, uphold the law. (1987)

2. Frankly, my dear, I don't give a damn. (1939)

3. You've got to ask yourself one question: 'Do I feel lucky?' Well, do ya, punk? (1971)

4. One morning I shot an elephant in my pyjamas. How he got in my pyjamas, I don't know. (1930)

5. I coulda had class. I coulda been a contender. I could've been somebody, instead of a bum, which is what I am. (1954)

6. Toto, I've a feeling we're not in Kansas anymore. (1939)

7. A boy's best friend is his mother. (1960)

8. Greed, for lack of a better word, is good. (1987)

9. All right, Mr. DeMille, I'm ready for my close-up. (1950)

10. Fasten your seatbelts. It's going to be a bumpy night. (1950)

THE MOVIE LOVER'S CHALLENGE

Release Date Challenge 6

Put these movies in order of their initial cinema release, starting with the oldest one.

1. The Revenant
    A Separation
    Once
    Amélie
    Children of Men

2. Inside Out
    The Artist
    The Royal Tenenbaums
    There Will Be Blood
    Inglourious Basterds

3. Crouching Tiger, Hidden Dragon
    City of God
    Donnie Darko
    Kill Bill: Vol 1
    The Tree of Life

THE MOVIE LOVER'S CHALLENGE

Movie Anagrams 6

Unscramble the letters to reveal the movie title.

1. brad to licking milk (1962 - Drama/ Mystey)

2. danny boned lice (1967 - Drama/ Crime)

3. robby ray seams (1968 - Horror/ Drama)

4. thing set (1973 - Comedy/ Drama)

5. there trend rue (1978 - War/ Drama)

6. in ale (1979 - Sci-fi/ Horror)

7. blurred anne (1982 - Sci-fi/ Action)

8. he pant then meal (1980 - Drama/ Historical Drama)

9. dang hi (1982 - Drama/ History)

10. skilled nightlife (1984 - Drama/ War)

THE MOVIE LOVER'S CHALLENGE

The Drama Diaries

1. In the movie "The Shawshank Redemption," what is the name of the main character played by Tim Robbins?
2. Who directed the 1993 drama "Schindler's List"?
3. Which acclaimed drama film follows the story of a young girl's life in Iran during and after the Islamic Revolution?
4. Who played the role of the mentally challenged man, Lennie Small, in the movie adaptation of John Steinbeck's novel "Of Mice and Men"?
5. Which 2014 drama film tells the story of a young drummer and his instructor who has no limits to make his student reacg their full potential?
6. What is the name of the dystopian drama film set in a future where emotions are suppressed through drugs, and a man stops taking the drugs, rediscovering his feelings?
7. In the movie "A Beautiful Mind," Russell Crowe portrayed which real-life Nobel laureate mathematician?
8. Which critically acclaimed drama movie follows the story of a transgender woman and her journey towards acceptance and self-discovery in 1920's Denmark?
9. Who directed the drama movie "Moonlight," which won the Academy Award for Best Picture in 2017?
10. Which drama film, directed by Darren Aronofsky, explores the intense and obsessive pursuit of perfection in the world of ballet?

THE MOVIE LOVER'S CHALLENGE

Roles on Roles 7

Can you name the actor who has appeared in each set of movies?

1. Step Brothers
   Between Two Ferns: The Movie
   Krampus
   lower

2. Secretary
   Crazy Heart
   Frank
   The Dark Knight

3. Me Before You
   Solo: A Star Wars Story
   Last Christmas
   Terminator Genisys

4. Three Billboards Outside Ebbing, Missouri
   Seven Psychopaths
   The Green Mile
   Moon

5. The Faculty
   The Texas Chainsaw Massacre; The Beginning
   Random Acts of Violence
   The Fast and the Furious

THE MOVIE LOVER'S CHALLENGE

Role Recall 7

Is it possible for you to name the actor and film by using the name of the character and the year in which the movie was released?

1. Dr Richard Kimble (1993)

2. Rose Dewitt Bukater (1997)

3. Natalie Cook (2000)

4. Korben Dallas (1997)

5. Johnny Utah (1991)

6. Atticus Finch (1962)

7. Dr Niko Tatopoulos (1998)

8. Norman Bates (1960)

9. Jack Burton (1986)

10. Neytiri (2009)

THE MOVIE LOVER'S CHALLENGE

Keeping It Vague 7

Can you guess the movie based on a vague description?

1. Amidst the harrowing backdrop of World War II, a man unexpectedly finds his moral compass challenged as he seeks to protect and save lives in the face of unspeakable atrocities, leading him on a path of unlikely heroism and sacrifice. Set in a tumultuous era, the film captures the journey of one individual's transformation from self-interest to profound empathy. (1993)

2. A captivating portrayal of life within a tight-knit criminal community, showcasing the rise and eventual unraveling of individuals entangled in loyalty, power struggles, and the allure of illicit riches. The narrative follows their journey from humble beginnings to the zenith of their criminal empire, only to be ensnared by the very web they helped weave. (1990)

3. In a remote wilderness, a person seeks solitude and encounters a tribe with a different way of life. As they become immersed in the tribe's culture, tensions arise, leading to a dramatic clash between two contrasting worlds. (1990)

THE MOVIE LOVER'S CHALLENGE

Complete The Title 7

Challenge yourself to fill in the missing word from these movie titles.

1. If _____ Street Could Talk (2018, Kik Layne)

2. Jojo _____ (2019, Roman Griffin Davis)

3. _____ Zhivago (1965, Omar Sharif)

4. Dead _____ Society (1989, Robin Williams)

5. Good _____ Hunting (1997, Robin Williams)

6. _____ Figures (2016, Taraji P Henson)

7. The _____ Game (2014, Benedict Cumberbatch)

8. Mad Max: _____ Road (2015, Tom Hardy)

9. _____ Swan (2010, Natalie Portman)

10. _____ Island (2010, Leonardo DiCaprio)

THE MOVIE LOVER'S CHALLENGE

Familiar Phrases 7

Can you identify the movie that first made these iconic quotes famous?

1. What we've got here is failure to communicate. (1967)

2. Love means never having to say you're sorry. (1970)

3. The stuff that dreams are made of. (1941)

4. They call me Mister Tibbs! (1967)

5. Rosebud. (1941)

6. Made it, Ma! Top of the worrld! (1949)

7. I'm as mad as hell, and I'm not going to take this anymore! (1976)

8. Louis, I think this is the beginnings of a beautiful friendship. (1942)

9. A census taker once tried to test me. I ate his liver with some fava beans and a nice Chianti. (1991)

10. I am big! It's the picture that got small. (1950)

THE MOVIE LOVER'S CHALLENGE

Release Date Challenge 7

Put these movies in order of their initial cinema release, starting with the oldest one.

1. The Green Mile
    Annie Hall
    The Breakfast Club
    Apocalypse Now
    Beverly Hills Cop

2. Platoon
    The Shining
    Toy Story
    E.T. the Extra-Terrestrial
    American Beauty

3. Forrest Gump
    The Farewell
    Shang-Chi and the Legend of the Ten Rings
    Downfall
    Whiplash

THE MOVIE LOVER'S CHALLENGE

Movie Anagrams 7

Unscramble the letters to reveal the movie title.

1. ant loop (1986 - War/ Drama)

2. eat scope toys died (1989 - Drama/ Teen)

3. fin over gun (1992 - Western/ Drama)

4. in it he then gets lap (1996 - Romance/ Drama)

5. go far (1996 - Crime/ Thriller)

6. sight be bowlike (1998 - Comedy/ Crime)

7. sumo sam aloft (2000 - Drama/ Comedy)

8. mr and the hit (1949 - Noir/ Thriller)

9. wear I drown (1954 - Thriller/ Mystery)

10. stride toys sew (1961 - Musical/ Romance)

THE MOVIE LOVER'S CHALLENGE

Lights, Camera, Laughter!

1. What is the name of the 1997 comedy movie where Jim Carrey's character has to tell the truth for 24 hours?
2. Which film features a duo of slackers who travel through time in a phone booth to complete their history report?
3. Which 1983 comedy film stars Eddie Murphy as a streetwise con artist who switches lives with a wealthy investment banker?
4. In the movie "Superbad," what are the first names of the two best friends who are determined to have an unforgettable night before graduating high school?
5. In the movie "The Hangover," the characters wake up after a wild night in which city?
6. In the movie "Groundhog Day", what song awakes Bill Murray's character every morning?
7. What is the name of the 1992 comedy film where the lead character poses as a nun to hide from mobsters?
8. Which comedy film stars Simon Pegg as a police officer assigned to a small English town with a dark secret?
9. In the film "Little Miss Sunshine," what talent does Olive Hoover perform at the beauty pageant?
10. What are the first names of the burglars in the 1990 Christmas movie "Home Alone"?

THE MOVIE LOVER'S CHALLENGE

Same Name, Different Faces 1

Identify the character portrayed by multiple actors across various movies.

1. Michael Caine -- Jeremy Irons -- Andy Serkis

2. Timothy Dalton -- Pierce Brosnan -- George Lazenby

3. Brian Cox -- Gaspard Ulliel -- Anthony Hopkins

4. Christopher Reeve -- Brandon Routh -- Henry Cavill

5. Robert Downey Jr. -- Christopher Plummer -- Ian McKellen

6. Tobey Maguire -- Andrew Garfield -- Tom Holland

7. Christopher Lee -- Gary Oldman -- Luke Evans

8. Zoe Kravitz -- Michelle Pfeiffer -- Anne Hathaway

9. Steve Martin -- Roger Moore -- Peter Sellers

10. Russell Crowe -- Kevin Costner -- Carey Elwes

THE MOVIE LOVER'S CHALLENGE

Role Recall 8

Is it possible for you to name the actor and film by using the name of the character and the year in which the movie was released?

1. Danny Ocean (2001)

2. Harry Stamper (1998)

3. Freddy Krueger (1984)

4. Amsterdam Vallon (2002)

5. Trinity (1999)

6. Hans Landa (2009)

7. Nina Sayers (2010)

8. Don Vito Corleone (1972)

9. Harvey Dent (2008)

10. Walter Sobchak (1998)

THE MOVIE LOVER'S CHALLENGE

Keeping It Vague 8

Can you guess the movie based on a vague description?

1. A tightly-knit group of talented individuals with a shared passion navigate personal struggles while preparing for a high-stakes competition that tests their skills and friendship. As tensions rise, the group must confront their inner demons and work together to achieve their harmonious dreams. (2012)

2. A group of diverse high school students find themselves in an unexpected situation, forced to spend a day together. As they navigate through personal struggles and reveal their hidden sides, deep connections form, leading to unexpected bonds and revelations about their shared humanity. (1985)

3. A middle-aged individual with a unique and secretive personal history becomes the subject of fascination for a group of acquaintances, leading to a series of increasingly funny and disturbing interactions that delve into the depths of their psyche. (2005)

THE MOVIE LOVER'S CHALLENGE

Roles on Roles 8

Can you name the actor who has appeared in each set of movies?

1. The Irishman
   House Of Gucci
   American Histler
   Kill Your Darlings

2. Before We Go
   Men in Black 3
   She's Out of My League
   Star Trek Into Darkness

3. Hello Carter
   Stardust
   Spider-Man: No Way Home
   The Theory of Everything

4. Die Hard 4.0
   10 Cloverfield Lane
   Scott Pilgrim vs. The World
   Birds Of Prey

5. The Double
   The Social Network
   Now You See Me
   Zombieland

THE MOVIE LOVER'S CHALLENGE

Complete The Title 8

Challenge yourself to fill in the missing word from these movie titles.

1. _____ by the Sea (2016, Casey Afleck)

2. Finding _____ (2003, Albert Brooks)

3. Snow _____ and the Seven Dwarfs (1937, Adriana Caselotti)

4. _____ Gems (2019, Adam Sandler)

5. The _____ of Navarone (1961, David Niven)

6. Blade Runner _____ (2017, Harrison Ford)

7. The _____ Suspects (1995, Kevin Spacey)

8. Ex _____ (2015, Alicia Vikander)

9. Dallas _____ Club (2013, Matthew McConaughey)

10. _____ Beauty (1959, Mary Costa)

THE MOVIE LOVER'S CHALLENGE

Familiar Phrases 8

Can you identify the movie that first made these iconic quotes famous?

1. Why don't you come up sometime and see me? (1933)

2. I want to be alone. (1932)

3. After all, tomorrow is another day! (1939)

4. Round up the usual suspects. (1942)

5. If you build it, he will come. (1989)

6. Take your stinking paws off me, you damned dirty ape. (1968)

7. They're here. (1982)

8. Is it safe. (1976)

9. Open the pod bay doors, please, HAL. (1968)

10. Toga! Toga! (1978)

THE MOVIE LOVER'S CHALLENGE

Release Date Challenge 8

Put these movies in order of their initial cinema release, starting with the oldest one.

1. Heat
   Skyfall
   Toy Story 4
   Minari
   The Gift

2. The Salesman
   Batman Returns
   The Lion King
   Good Time
   Catch Me If You Can

3. One Night in Miami
   Birdman
   Fear and Loathing in Las Vegas
   Princess Mononoke
   The Tragedy of Macbeth

THE MOVIE LOVER'S CHALLENGE

Movie Anagrams 8

Unscramble the letters to reveal the movie title.

1. casey tanned duck stub sic hand hid (1969 - Western/ Drama)

2. haste pilot sure witch (1971 - Drama)

3. ever nice lad (1972 - Adventure/ Drama)

4. win hot can (1974 - Mystery/ Drama)

5. hall vines (1975 - Musical/ Drama)

6. burn all gig (1980 - Drama/ Sport)

7. do boast (1981 - War/ Drama)

8. so tie to (1982 - Comedy/ Romance)

9. purer pole cloth (1985 - Drama/ Historical Drama)

10. eve bull vet (1986 - Mystery/ Drama)

THE MOVIE LOVER'S CHALLENGE

Role Recall 9

Is it possible for you to name the actor and film by using the name of the character and the year in which the movie was released?

1. Keyser Söze (1995)

2. Randle McMurphy (1975)

3. Katniss Everdeen (2012)

4. Ethan Hunt (1996)

5. Andy Dufresne (1994)

6. Morticia Addams (1991)

7. Rick Blaine (1942)

8. Kevin McCallister (1990)

9. Simon Phoenix (1993)

10. Christian Grey (2015)

THE MOVIE LOVER'S CHALLENGE

Dogs on Film

1. What is the name of the dog in the movie "The Mask" starring Jim Carrey?
2. In the 2004 comedy "Anchorman: The Legend of Ron Burgundy," what is the name of Ron Burgundy's dog?
3. What breed of dog is Beethoven in the movie franchise of the same name?
4. How many puppies did Perdita give birth to in the 1961 animated classic "101 Dalmatians"?
5. What is the name of the dog with a unique pattern on his fur who believes he has superpowers?
6. Which Wes Anderson film features a pack of dogs and a young boy on a quest to find his lost pet?
7. In the film "Turner & Hooch," what breed of dog is Hooch?
8. In the movie "The Wizard of Oz," what is the name of Dorothy's loyal dog who accompanies her on her journey to Oz?
9. What is the name of the dog in the movie "Coco," who helps Miguel navigate the Land of the Dead?
10. What is the name of John Connor's dog in the movie "Terminator 2: Judgment Day"?

THE MOVIE LOVER'S CHALLENGE

Keeping It Vague 9

Can you guess the movie based on a vague description?

1. A secretary encounters a mysterious opportunity at a secluded motel while on the run, leading to a series of unsettling events that unveil the disturbing secrets hidden within the establishment's walls. As her curiosity deepens, she becomes entangled in a psychological web of deception, fear, and unexpected revelations. (1960)

2. A resilient individual finds themselves marooned in an inhospitable environment, using their wits and expertise to survive while facing numerous challenges and setbacks. As the situation escalates, their struggle for survival becomes a test of mental fortitude and resourcefulness. (2015)

3. In a gritty exploration of human psyche, a tormented individual embarks on a harrowing journey into a war-torn land, descending into madness as he confronts the darkness within himself and the chaotic horrors of the conflict around him. As the line between reality and delusion blurs, he grapples with the haunting realization that the true battle might be the one waged within his own mind. (1979)

THE MOVIE LOVER'S CHALLENGE

Family Film Frenzy

1. In the movie "The Incredibles," what is the name of the supervillain who disguises himself as a hero to manipulate public opinion against superheroes?
2. Which 2009 stop-motion animated film features the voice talents of Dakota Fanning, Teri Hatcher, and Keith David, and follows a young girl who discovers an alternate world that mirrors her own?
3. In the film "E.T. the Extra-Terrestrial," what is the first name of Elliott's little sister, who forms a close bond with the friendly alien?
4. The movie "The Secret of NIMH" centres around a group of intelligent and escaped laboratory rats. What does NIMH stand for?
5. In "The Lion King," what type of animal is the wise and colourful character Zazu?
6. What is the name of the puppet maker who creates Pinocchio?
7. What is the name of the young boy who befriends a friendly alien robot in the film "The Iron Giant"?
8. How much does it cost to feed the bird in "Mary Poppins"?
9. Which classic family film features a character named Fizzgig, a small, fluffy creature that accompanies the main protagonists on their journey?
10. In the film "Honey, I Shrunk the Kids," what is the name of the device that Wayne Szalinski invents, leading to the kids being shrunk?

THE MOVIE LOVER'S CHALLENGE

Complete The Title 9

Challenge yourself to fill in the missing word from these movie titles.

1. Call Me By _____ Name (2017, Timothee Chalamet)

2. The _____ King (1994, Matthew Broderick)

3. Straight Outta _____ (2015, O'Shea Jackson Jr)

4. A _____ is Born (2018, Lady Gaga)

5. Little _____ (1994, Susan Sarandon)

6. _____ to Busan (2016, Gong Yoo)

7. Bohemian _____ (2018, Rami Malek)

8. _____ Thread (2017, Daniel Day-Lewis)

9. _____ Grade (2018, Eslie Fisher)

10. Sorry to _____ You (2018, LaKeith Stanfield)

THE MOVIE LOVER'S CHALLENGE

Familiar Phrases 9

Can you identify the movie that first made these iconic quotes famous?

1. My precious. (2002)

2. Nobody puts Baby in a corner. (1987)

3. I need your clothes, your boots, and your motorcycle. (1991)

4. Get in, loser. We're going shopping. (2004)

5. All those moments will be lost in time, like tears in rain. (1982)

6. I like you very much. Just as you are. (2001)

7. By all means, move at a glacial pace. You know how that thrills me. (2006)

8. Every time a bell rings, an angel gets its wings. (1946)

9. That'll do, pig. That'll do. (1995)

10. Life moves pretty fast. If you don't stop and look around once in a while, you could miss it. (1986)

THE MOVIE LOVER'S CHALLENGE

Release Date Challenge 9

Put these movies in order of their initial cinema release, starting with the oldest one.

1. The 'Burbs
   The Hunt for the Wilderpeople
   Gremlins
   The Sting
   The X-Files

2. The Incredibles
   The Other Guys
   Hostel
   The Untouchables
   Watchmen

3. No Time to Die
   The Princess Bride
   Batman Begins
   A Star Is Born
   Blade Runner 2049

THE MOVIE LOVER'S CHALLENGE

Movie Anagrams 9

Unscramble the letters to reveal the movie title.

1. relax a day fog saint hug (2014 - Sci-fi/ Action)

2. i jolt a heat bin (1969 - Crime/ Action)

3. score podlet (2019 - Horror/ Thriller)

4. i raw moo hit wave (1985 - Romance/ Drama)

5. righten crawl (2014 - Crime/ Thriller)

6. streams the bud (1955 - War/ Action)

7. bad mud bun derm (1994 - Comedy)

8. hay deaf doted (1985 - Horror/ Sci-fi)

9. stripe he get (2006 - Sci-fi/ Drama)

10. a liced may cope (1984 - Comedy/ Crime)

THE MOVIE LOVER'S CHALLENGE

Same Name, Different Faces 2

Identify the character portrayed by multiple actors across various movies.

1. Mads Mikkelsen -- Jamie Campbell Bower -- Johnny Depp

2. Val Kilmer -- George Clooney -- Ben Affleck

3. Cary Elwes -- Rusell Crowe -- Errol Flynn

4. Greer Garson -- Keira Knightley -- Lily James

5. Kenneth Branagh -- Albert Finney -- Peter Ustinov

6. Lily James -- Anna Kendrick -- Camila Cabello

7. Christopher Lambert -- Casper Van Dien -- Miles O'Keeffe

8. Alec Baldwin -- Harrison Ford -- Ben Affleck

9. Matt Salinger -- Chris Evans -- Reb Brown

10. Edward Norton -- Eric Bana -- Mark Ruffalo

THE MOVIE LOVER'S CHALLENGE

Role Recall 10

Is it possible for you to name the actor and film by using the name of the character and the year in which the movie was released?

1. Stanley Ipkiss (1994)

2. Captain Steven Hiller (1996)

3. Wayne Szalinski (1989)

4. Gracie Hart (2000)

5. Ann Darrow (2005)

6. Jack Slater (1993)

7. Scarlett O'Hara (1939)

8. Dr King Schultz (2012)

9. Elle Woods (2001)

10. Dorothy Gale (1939)

THE MOVIE LOVER'S CHALLENGE

Keeping It Vague 10

Can you guess the movie based on a vague description?

1. In a simmering urban neighborhood on a sweltering summer day, tensions escalate between diverse residents, highlighting the complexities of race, culture, and societal pressures. As the day unfolds, a seemingly trivial incident triggers a series of events that push the community to confront deep-seated prejudices and erupt in a climactic confrontation. (1989)

2. In a gritty urban setting, a charismatic duo forms an unlikely partnership as they navigate the fast-paced world of underground street basketball tournaments, combining their unique skills to challenge stereotypes and overcome personal struggles. As they hustle their way through intense games and comedic mishaps, their journey explores themes of friendship, self-discovery, and the power of collaboration. (1992)

3. In a quiet suburban town, an eccentric inventor's unfinished creation with an unusual physical condition is discovered and brought into the community, leading to both admiration and fear as his talents bring remarkable changes to the lives of the locals. As relationships develop and tensions rise, the protagonist's extraordinary abilities ultimately collide with the ordinary world around him. (1990)

THE MOVIE LOVER'S CHALLENGE

Complete The Title 10

Challenge yourself to fill in the missing word from these movie titles.

1. Winter's _____ (2010, Jennifer Lawrence)

2. _____ Holiday (1953, Gregory Peck)

3. _____ Hood (2010, Russell Crowe)

4. Eternal Sunshine of the _____ Mind (2004, Jim Carrey)

5. _____ Park (1993, Sam Neill)

6. Invasion of the _____ Snatchers (1978, Donald Sutherland)

7. The _____ Artist (2017, James Franco)

8. _____ at Tiffany's (1967, Audrey Hepburn)

9. _____ Girl (2014, Ben Affleck)

10. The Big _____ (1998, Jeff Bridges)

THE MOVIE LOVER'S CHALLENGE

Roles on Roles 9

Can you name the actor who has appeared in each set of movies?

1. Knight of Cups
   Immortals
   Rise of the Planet of The Apes
   Slumdog Millionaire

2. In Good Company
   Spider-Man 3
   Traffic
   BlacKkKlansman

3. The Social Network
   Tag
   Celeste & Jesse Forever
   I Love You. Man

4. Rushmore
   The Darjeeling Limited
   Moonrise Kingdom
   Saving Mr. Banks

5. Lars and the Real Girl
   Mary Poppins Returns
   Match Point
   Transsiberian

THE MOVIE LOVER'S CHALLENGE

Familiar Phrases 10

Can you identify the movie that first made these iconic quotes famous?

1. Bury me in the ocean with my ancestors that jumped from the ships...because they knew death was better than bondage. (2018)

2. Get busy livin' or get busy dyin'...That's goddamn right. (1994)

3. But did you die? (2011)

4. My name is Inigo Montoya. You killed my father. Prepare to die. (1987)

5. Ernest Hemingway once wrote, 'The world is a fine place and worth fighting for.' I agree with the second part. (1995)

6. You either die a hero or live long enough to see yourself become the villain. (2008)

7. To live would be an awfully big adventure. (1991)

8. Carpe diem. Seize the day, boys. Make your lives extraordinary. (1989)

9. Now we are free. I will see you again, but not yet. Not yet. (2000)

10. I love you 3000. (2019)

THE MOVIE LOVER'S CHALLENGE

Release Date Challenge 10

Put these movies in order of their initial cinema release, starting with the oldest one.

1. Easy Rider
   Wedding Crashers
   Black Mass
   Frozen
   Edge of Tomorrow

2. Enemy of The State
   Captain America: The First Avenger
   Trading Places
   Cloudy with a Chance of Meatballs
   Labyrinth

3. Swiss Army Man
   Alita: Battle Angel
   The Notebook
   When Harry Met Sally
   The Revenant

THE MOVIE LOVER'S CHALLENGE

Movie Anagrams 10

Unscramble the letters to reveal the movie title.

1. cherry choke throws prior out (1975 - Musical/ Horror)

2. a bar eel bunk (2000 - Thriller/ Sci-fi)

3. roughed tattooers (1988 - Comedy/ Slapstick)

4. how can a mouse catch led fat billy (2009 - Family/ Comedy)

5. bally leg do len (2001 - Comedy/ Romance)

6. far doped dred (1991 - Fantasy/ Comedy)

7. shared draws sin cods (1990 - Fantasy/ Romance)

8. i jam me floor twister (2006 - War/ Drama)

9. you suck ton (2003 - Comedy)

10. newel halo (1978 - Horror/ Thriller)

THE MOVIE LOVER'S CHALLENGE

Movie Villains

Can you name the first movie that these villains appeared in?

1. Nurse Ratched

2. Annie Wilkes

3. Hans Gruber

4. Leatherface

5. Patrick Bateman

6. Alex Forrest

7. Miranda Priestly

8. Ernst Stavro Blofeld

9. Alex DeLarge

10. Travis Bickle

THE MOVIE LOVER'S CHALLENGE

Roles on Roles 10

Can you name the actor who has appeared in each set of movies?

1. Midnight In Oaris -- Frost/ Nixon -- Masters of Sex -- The Queen

2. The Guest -- Beauty and the Beast -- I'm Your Man -- Blithe Spirit

3. Tom & Jerry: The Movie -- If I Stay -- Let Me In -- Kick-Ass

4. Spring Breakers -- Pineapple Express -- The Disaster Artist -- 127 Hours

5. Thirteen -- Whatever Works -- The Wrestler -- The Ides Of March

THE MOVIE LOVER'S CHALLENGE

Famous Voices 1

Identify the characters voiced by these actors in the given movies.

1. Robin Williams (Ferngully: The Last Rainforest)

2. Will Smith (Shark Tale)

3. Owen Wilson (Cars)

4. John Goodman (Monsters, Inc.)

5. Angela Lansbury (Beauty and the Beast)

6. James Woods (Hercules)

7. Jerry Seinfeld (Bee Movie)

8. Eddie Murphy (Mulan)

9. John Lithgow (Shrek)

10. Jeremy Irons (The Lion King)

THE MOVIE LOVER'S CHALLENGE

Direct Orders 1

Arrange the movies directed by these famous directors in chronological order of their release, from oldest to most recent.

1. James Cameron
    Titanic
    Avatar
    Terminator 2: Judgment Day
    Aliens
    The Abyss

2. Ridley Scott
    Alien
    Blade Runner
    Gladiator
    The Martian
    Black Hawk Down

3. Steven Spielberg
    Jaws
    E.T. the Extra-Terrestrial
    Jurassic Park
    Saving Private Ryan
    Raiders Of The Lost Ark

4. Christopher Nolan
    Inception
    The Dark Knight
    Interstellar
    Dunkirk
    Memento

THE MOVIE LOVER'S CHALLENGE

Famous Voices 2

Identify the characters voiced by these actors in the given movies.

1. Tim Allen (Toy Story)

2. Jim Parsons (Home)

3. Sylvester Stallone (Antz)

4. Denis Leary (A Bug's Life)

5. Beyoncé (Epic)

6. Mel Gibson (Pocahontas)

7. Kelsey Grammer (Toy Story 2)

8. Chris Pratt (The Lego Movie)

9. Bill Hader (Cloudy With A Chance Of Meatballs)

10. Brad Pitt (Megamind)

THE MOVIE LOVER'S CHALLENGE

Roles on Roles 11

Can you name the actor who has appeared in each set of movies?

1. Bad Moms -- Anchorman: The Legend of Ron Burgundy -- Going The Distance -- Don't Tell Mom The Babysitter's Dead

2. That Thing You Do! -- Harold & Kumar Get the Munchies -- Can't Hardly Wait -- Sweet Home Alabama

3. Belle -- Beyond the Lights -- Concussion -- Beauty and the Beast

4. Glory Road -- Sweet Home Alabama -- The Lincoln Lawyer -- The Forever Purge

5. The Help -- Pete's Dragon -- Rocketman -- Jurassic World

THE MOVIE LOVER'S CHALLENGE

Direct Orders 2

Arrange the movies directed by these famous directors in chronological order of their release, from oldest to most recent.

1. **Stanley Kubrick**
    2001: A Space Odyssey
    A Clockwork Orange
    The Shining
    Full Metal Jacket
    Barry Lyndon

2. **Alfred Hitchcock**
    Psycho
    Rear Window
    Vertigo
    North By Northwest
    The Birds

3. **Martin Scorcese**
    Goodfellas
    Taxi Driver
    Raging Bull
    The Departed
    Casino

4. **Quentin Tarantino**
    Pulp Fiction
    Reservoir Dogs
    Kill Bill: Volume 1
    Inglorious Basterds
    Django Unchained

THE MOVIE LOVER'S CHALLENGE

Blockbuster Brawls

1. In the movie "Die Hard," what building is taken over by terrorists?
2. Who plays the iconic role of John Wick in the action film series of the same name?
3. What is the name of the main villain in the James Bond film "Skyfall" played by Javier Bardem?
4. In the movie "Kill Bill: Volume 1," what is the code name of the protagonist played by Uma Thurman?
5. Who directed the action-packed movie "Mad Max: Fury Road" released in 2015?
6. What is the name of the futuristic city protected by Judge Dredd in the movie adaptation of the comic book?
7. What is the name of Tom Cruise's character in the Mission: Impossible franchise?
8. What is the title of the action film where Dwayne Johnson plays a primatologist trying to save a rare albino gorilla from genetic experiments?
9. In the movie "Gladiator," who plays the role of the young Roman Emperor Commodus?
10. Who wrote and directed the action film the Kill Bill movies?

THE MOVIE LOVER'S CHALLENGE

Famous Voices 3

Identify the characters voiced by these actors in the given movies.

1. Craig T. Nelson (The Incredibles)

2. Will Smith (Spies In Disguise)

3. Tom Holland (Onward)

4. Sam Elliott (The Good Dinosaur)

5. Michael Keaton (Cars)

6. Christopher Walken (Antz)

7. Simon Pegg (Ice Age: Dawn of the Dinosaurs)

8. Gerard Butler (How to Train Your Dragon)

9. Amy Poehler (Inside Out)

10. Josh Gad (Frozen)

THE MOVIE LOVER'S CHALLENGE

Direct Orders 3

Arrange the movies directed by these famous directors in chronological order of their release, from oldest to most recent.

1. **Francis Ford Coppola**
    The Godfather
    Apocalypse Now
    The Conversation
    Runble Fish
    Patton

2. **Akira Kurosawa**
    Seven Samurai
    Rashomon
    Yojimbo
    Throne Of Blood
    Ran

3. **David Fincher**
    Se7en
    Fight Club
    The Social Network
    Gone Girl
    Zodiac

4. **Wes Anderson**
    The Royal Tenenbaums
    Moonrise Kingdom
    The Grand Budapest Hotel
    Fantastic Mr. Fox
    Rushmorre

THE MOVIE LOVER'S CHALLENGE

Roles on Roles 12

Can you name the actor who has appeared in each set of movies?

1. High Rise -- Dracula Untold -- Beauty and the Beast -- Fast & Furious 6

2. Source Code -- Kiss Kiss Bang Bang -- Pixels -- Gone Baby Gone

3. Terminator Salvation -- Hacksaw Ridge -- Clash of the Titans -- Avatar

4. Chicago -- Charlie's Angels -- Kill Bill: Vol.1 -- The Trouble with Bliss

5. Jackie Brown -- Joy -- Joker -- Taxi Driver

THE MOVIE LOVER'S CHALLENGE

Movie Taglines 1

Challenge yourself to identify the films behind these iconic taglines.

1. In space, no one can hear you scream. (1979 - Sci-fi/ Horror)

2. You'll believe a man can fly. (1978 - Sci-fi/ Action)

3. Fear can hold you prisoner. Hope can set you free. (1994 - Drama/ Crime)

4. The story of a lifetime. (1994 - Drama/ Romance)

5. There can be only one. (1986 - Action/ Fantasy)

6. Something went wrong in the lab today. Very wrong. (1986 - Horror/ Sci-fi)

7. Getting back was only the beginning. (1989 - Sci-fi/ Adventure)

8. In the heart of the nation's capital, in a courthouse of the U.S. government, one man will stop at nothing to keep his honor, and one will stop at nothing to find the truth. (1992 - Legal drama/ Thriller)

9. From a dimension beyond the living, a terror to scare you to death. (1982 - Horror/ Fantasy)

10. You'll never go in the water again! (1975 - Adventure/ Thriller)

THE MOVIE LOVER'S CHALLENGE

Direct Orders 4

Arrange the movies directed by these famous directors in chronological order of their release, from oldest to most recent.

1. **Clint Eastwood**
    Unforgiven
    Million Dollar Baby
    Mystic River
    Gran Torino
    Flags Of Our Fathers

2. **Guillermo Del Toro**
    Pan's Labyrinth
    The Shape Of Water
    Crimson Peak
    Hellboy
    Pacific Rim

3. **Tim Burton**
    Edward Scissorhands
    Beetlejuice
    Batman
    Corpse Bride
    Big Fish

4. **Sofia Coppola**
    Lost In Translation
    The Virgin Suicides
    Marie Antionette
    Somewhere
    The Bling Ring

THE MOVIE LOVER'S CHALLENGE

Movie Taglines 2

Challenge yourself to identify the films behind these iconic taglines.

1. The man in the hat is back... (1984 - Adventure/ Action)

2. The Legend Comes to Life. (2001 - Fantasy/ Adventure)

3. Spartans, tonight, we dine in hell! (2006 - Action/ War)

4. Man Has Made His Match... Now It's His Problem. (1982 - Sci-fi/ Action)

5. 71% of the Earth's surface is covered by water. That's a lot of space to find one fish. (2003 - Family/ Adventure)

6. Life finds a way. (1993 - Sci-fi/ Adventure)

7. Failure is not an option. (1995 - Drama/ History)

8. Honk if you love Brian. (1979 - Comedy/ Satire)

9. No spook, specter, or haunt will ever be safe again. (1984 - Comedy/ Fantasy)

10. There is a place you can escape your past, as long as you follow every rule. (2019 - Thriller/ Drama)

THE MOVIE LOVER'S CHALLENGE

Direct Orders 5

Arrange the movies directed by these famous directors in chronological order of their release, from oldest to most recent.

1. **Orson Welles**
   Citizen Kane
   The Magnificent Andersons
   Touch Of Evil
   The Lady From Shanghai
   Chimes Of Midnight

2. **Spike Lee**
   Do The Right Thing
   Malcolm X
   BlacKkKlansman
   25th Hour
   Jungle Fever

3. **Ang Lee**
   Crouching Tiger, Hidden Dragon
   Brokeback Mountain
   Life Of Pi
   Sense and Sensibility
   Lust, Caution

4. **Kathryn Bigelow**
   The Hurt Locker
   Zero Dark Thirty
   Point Break
   Near Dark
   Detroit

THE MOVIE LOVER'S CHALLENGE

Movie Taglines 3

Challenge yourself to identify the films behind these iconic taglines.

1. Earth. It Was Fun While It Lasted. (1998 - Sci-fi/ Action)

2. His scars run deep. (1990 - Fantasy/ Romance)

3. Come in close, because the more you think you see, the easier it'll be to fool you (2013 - Thriller/ Crime)

4. Feathers will Fly! (2000 - Adventure/ Family)

5. He was the perfect weapon until he became the target. (2002 - Action/ Thriller)

6. Heroes aren't born. They're built. (2008 - Action/ Sci-fi)

7. Somewhere out there, it may all be happening right now. (1977 - Sci-fi/ Adventure)

8. The list is life. The man was real. The story is true. (1993 - War/ Drama)

9. One choice can transform you. (2014 - Sci-fi/Action)

10. Discover the past, live the present, fight the future. (1998 - Sci-fi/ Drama)

THE MOVIE LOVER'S CHALLENGE

Many Names, Same Face 1

Identify the actor who portrayed all these characters.

1. Detective Jimmy Shaker -- Ken Mattingly -- George Milton -- Burt Hammersmith -- Lieutenant Dan Taylor

2. Suzanne Vale -- Joanna Kramer -- Gail Hartman -- Madeline Ashton -- Margaret Thatcher

3. Jack Saunders -- Gavin Verheek -- Paul Davenport -- John Pierce -- Peter McCallister

4. George Malley -- Woody Stevens -- Chili Palmer -- Edna Turnblad -- Sean Archer

5. Daniel Plainview -- Danny Flynn -- Christy Brown -- Bill "The Butcher" Cutting -- Abraham Lincoln

THE MOVIE LOVER'S CHALLENGE

Movie Taglines 4

Challenge yourself to identify the films behind these iconic taglines.

1. The story of a man with a free soul...and with the courage to follow it. (1995 - War/ Drama)

2. Mankind was born on Earth. It was never meant to die here. (2014 - Sci-fi/ Adventure)

3. You know the name. You know the number. (1995 - Action/ Adventure)

4. The Mission Begins 05:05:06 (2006 - Action/ Adventure)

5. The Legend Begins. (2005 - Action/ Fantasy)

6. Free your mind. (1999 - Action/ Sci-fi)

7. Your mind is the scene of the crime. (2010 - Action/ Sci-fi)

8. A homespun murder story. (1996 - Crime/ Thriller)

9. One wrong flight can ruin your whole day. (1997 - Action/ Thriller)

10. If you see only one movie this year...you ought to get out more often. (1988 - Comedy/ Action)

THE MOVIE LOVER'S CHALLENGE

Many Names, Same Face 2

Identify the actor who portrayed all these characters.

1. Angelo Provolone -- Captain Ray Quick -- Barney Ross -- Ray Breslin -- John J Rambo

2. Roger Ferris -- Dom Cobb -- Jim Carroll -- Jordan Belfort -- Jack Dawson

3. Rosalyn Rosenfeld -- Joy Mangano -- Tiffany Maxwell -- Mystique -- Katniss Everdeen

4. Frank Pierce -- Tom Welles -- Ben Gates -- Memphis Raines -- Castor Troy

5. Will Randall -- Daryl Van Horne -- Randle McMurphy -- Colonel Nathan Jessup -- Jack Torrance

THE MOVIE LOVER'S CHALLENGE

Roles on Roles 13

Can you name the actor who has appeared in each set of movies?

1. Predators -- Repo Man -- Elysium -- I Am Legend

2. Snowden -- Mother's Day -- Die Hard 4.0 -- Hitman

3. Gerald's Game -- American Gangster -- San Andreas -- Watchmen

4. The Strangers -- The Captive -- Barefoot -- Underworld

5. 12 Years a Slave -- Run -- Glass -- Ocean's Eight

THE MOVIE LOVER'S CHALLENGE

Fright Night Flicks

1. What is the name of the iconic serial killer in the "Halloween" movie franchise?
2. Which horror movie features a group of friends who accidentally unleash ancient demons after playing a mysterious audio recording in a cabin in the woods?
3. What is the name of the demon that possesses Regan MacNeil in the classic horror film "The Exorcist"?
4. What is the name of the hotel that serves as the eerie setting for Stanley Kubrick's "The Shining"?
5. Which horror film features a mysterious videotape that curses anyone who watches it, leading to their death within seven days?
6. In the movie "A Nightmare on Elm Street" (1984), what is the name of the sinister and dream-haunting character played by Robert Englund?
7. Which horror film was inspired by the real-life case of the Perron family and their haunting experiences in their farmhouse in the 1970s?
8. In the horror classic "Rosemary's Baby" (1968), who portrays the role of Rosemary Woodhouse, the pregnant woman experiencing strange occurrences in her apartment building?
9. Which horror movie explores the terrifying consequences of an alien organism that assimilates and imitates other life forms in an Antarctic research station?
10. What is the name of the leader of the Cenobites in the Hellraiser series?

THE MOVIE LOVER'S CHALLENGE

Movie Taglines 5

Challenge yourself to identify the films behind these iconic taglines.

1. Nothing is real, everything is possible. (2009 - Sci-fi/ Drama)

2. An epic of epic epicness. (2010 - Action/ Comedy)

3. There's something about your first piece. (1999 - Comedy/ Teen)

4. Just because you're invited, doesn't mean you're welcome. (2017 - Horror/ Mystery)

5. There was only one man left in the family, and the mission was to save him. (1998 - War/ Drama)

6. The untold story behind the legend. (2010 - Adventure/ Action)

7. Behind every great love is a great story. (2004 - Romance/ Drama)

8. Let the games begin! (2004 - Horror/ Thriller)

9. For seven strangers, this is just the beginning of an exotic adventure. (2011 - Comedy/ Drama)

10. Shoot first. Sightsee later. (2008 - Comedy/ Crime)

THE MOVIE LOVER'S CHALLENGE

Many Names, Same Face 3

Identify the actor who portrayed all these characters.

1. John Kruger -- Ben Richards -- John Kimble -- Jack Slater -- Julius Benedict

2. Charlie Baileygates -- Ernie "Chip" Douglas -- Lloyd Christmas -- Bruce Nolan -- Stanley Ipkiss

3. Paul Vitti -- Carl Van Loon -- Victor Tellegio -- Jack Byrnes -- Vito Corleone

4. Chuck Noland -- Sam Baldwin -- Joe Banks -- Josh Baskin -- Paul Edgecomb

5. Dr. Jerome Davenport -- Troy Maxson -- Joe Miller -- John W. Creasy -- Ben Marco

THE MOVIE LOVER'S CHALLENGE

Movie Taglines 6

Challenge yourself to identify the films behind these iconic taglines.

1. One dream. Four Jamaicans. Twenty below zero. (1993 - Sports/ Comedy)

2. She just kept swimming... (2016 - Family/ Adventure)

3. When patriots become heroes. (2011 - Action/ Adventure)

4. Time is the enemy. (2019 - War/ Drama)

5. A whole new speed of hero. (2020 - Adventure/ Comedy)

6. In a place we hold dear, where wonder once lived... but soon from above, a new story begins. (2018 - Fantasy/ Family)

7. Warning: Exposing the Truth May Be Hazardous (1999 - Drama/ Thriller)

8. Don't get mad. Get everything. (1996 - Comedy/ Drama)

9. A boy who needs a friend finds a world that needs a hero. (1984 - Fantasy/ Family)

10. One man is Judge, Jury, AND Executioner. (1995 - Sci-fi/ Action)

THE MOVIE LOVER'S CHALLENGE

The Real Name Game 1

Can you name the star from their birth name?

1. Thomas Cruise Mapother IV

2. Mary Louise Streep

3. Emily Jean Stone

4. Natalie Hershlag

5. Caryn Elaine Johnson

6. Eric Marlon Bishop

7. Joaquin Rafael Bottom

8. Nicolas Kim Coppola

9. William Bradley Pitt

10. Norma Jean Mortenson

THE MOVIE LOVER'S CHALLENGE

Many Names, Same Face 4

Identify the actor who portrayed all these characters.

1. Lorraine Broughton -- Ravenna -- Meredith Vickers -- Cipher -- Imperator Furiosa

2. Jack Trainer -- Cliff Booth -- John Smith -- Jeffrey Goines -- Billy Beane

3. Elise Clifton-Ward -- Fox -- Christine Collins -- Thena -- Evelyn Salt

4. Will Caster -- Barnabas Collins -- Mort Rainey -- Grindelwald -- Tonto

5. Lt. Col. Frank Slade -- Tony D'Amato -- Big Boy Caprice -- Lefty -- Michael Corleone

THE MOVIE LOVER'S CHALLENGE

Movie Taglines 7

Challenge yourself to identify the films behind these iconic taglines.

1. The Oddest Couple Ever Unleashed! (1989 - Comedy/ Crime)

2. One man's struggle to take it easy. (1986 - Comedy/ Drama)

3. Great friends. Terrible choices. (2017 - Comedy/ Dark Comedy)

4. Crime is a disease. Meet the cure. (1986 - Action/ Crime)

5. Who puts the GLAD in GLADIATOR? (1997 - Adventure/ Musical)

6. It started like any other night. (2004 - Thriller/ Action)

7. Mighty Miracle Show Of 1000 Delights! (1939 - Musical/ Fantasy)

8. They're closer than you think. (2011 - Family/ Comedy)

9. The most magical one of all! (1971 - Musical/ Family)

10. It looks like a scam... but it's more than that... It's also a family affair. (2019 - Thriller/ Drama)

THE MOVIE LOVER'S CHALLENGE

Roles on Roles 14

Can you name the actor who has appeared in each set of movies?

1. Dunkirk -- Inception -- RocknRolla – Warrior

2. 10,000 BC -- When a Stranger Calls -- Open Road -- The American Side

3. Selma -- The Girl Before -- Peter Rabbit 2: The Runaway -- Don't Let Go

4. Get a Job -- Promising Young Woman -- Somebody I Used to Know -- The Lego Movie

5. The Devil's Double -- Captain America: The First Avenger -- The Duchess -- Warcraft: The Beginning

THE MOVIE LOVER'S CHALLENGE

The Real Name Game 2

Can you name the star from their birth name?

1. Destiny Hope Cyrus

2. Maurice Joseph Micklewhite

3. Edward Thomas Hardy

4. John Adedayo Bamidele Adegboyega

5. Alicia Christian Foster

6. Brianne Sidonie Desaulniers

7. Helen Lydia Mironoff

8. Diane Hall

9. Julie Anne Smith

10. Ronald Walken

THE MOVIE LOVER'S CHALLENGE

True Stories

1. Who played the role of Erin Brockovich in the 2000 movie based on her true story?
2. What 2013 movie tells the story of Ron Woodroof, an AIDS patient who smuggled unapproved drugs into the U.S. to treat fellow patients?
3. Who directed the 2010 true story movie "The Social Network," based on the creation of Facebook?
4. Which true story movie tells the tale of the first Jamaican bobsled team's journey to the Winter Olympics?
5. Which movie chronicles the true life of Chris Gardner, a struggling salesman who becomes a successful stockbroker?
6. In the movie "Catch Me If You Can," which actor played the role of Frank Abagnale, a con artist and forger?
7. Which sport is the centre of the true story of Michael Oher, a homeless boy who strives to be his best and become a professionial?
8. Whose story is depicted in the movie "The Theory of Everything"?
9. The movie "Hidden Figures" revolves around a group of African-American women who work for what company?
10. Which true story movie follows the life of boxer Jake LaMotta and his tumultuous career inside and outside the ring?

THE MOVIE LOVER'S CHALLENGE

Many Names, Same Face 5

Identify the actor who portrayed all these characters.

1. Marion Loxley -- Irina Spalko -- Galadriel -- Katharine Hepburn -- Florence Zimmerman

2. Dr. Alex Cross -- God -- Azeem -- Thaddeus Bradley -- Lucius Fox

3. Skeeter Phelan -- Wichita -- Allison Vandermeersh -- Billie Jean King -- Mia

4. Nina Sayers -- Anne Boleyn -- Jackie Kennedy -- Taffy Dale -- Jane Foster

5. Henry Brogan -- Chris Gardner -- Del Spooner -- Robert Clayton Dean -- Capt. Steven Hiller

THE MOVIE LOVER'S CHALLENGE

Movie Taglines 8

Challenge yourself to identify the films behind these iconic taglines.

1. When he said 'I do,' he never said what he did. (1994 - Comedy/ Action)
2. What we do in life echoes in eternity. (2000 - Action/ Adventure)
3. Discover the Side of Superheroes You've Never Seen Before. (2004 - Family/ Adventure)
4. Collide with destiny. (1997 - Romance/ Adventure)
5. Beyond darkness... beyond desolation... lies the greatest danger of all. (2013 - Adventure/ Family)
6. On The Road Of Life, There Are Old Friends, New Friends, And Stories That Change You. (2019 - Family/ Adventure)
7. Love is a force of nature. (2005 - Romance/ Drama)
8. Your future is in its hands. (1984 - Sci-fi/ Action)
9. Here's to the fools who dream. (2016 - Musical/ Romance)
10. A true story of a real fake. (2013 - Crime/ Drama)

THE MOVIE LOVER'S CHALLENGE

Many Names, Same Face 6

Identify the actor who portrayed all these characters.

1. Vivian Ward -- Dr. Rachel Mannus -- Julianne Potter -- Tinkerbell -- Alice Sutton

2. Janet Leigh -- Kelly Foster -- Mary Boleyn -- Olivia Wenscombe -- Natasha Romanoff

3. Jim Preston -- Barley Lightfoot -- Emmet Brickowski -- Owen Grady -- Peter Quill

4. President James Marshall -- Jack Ryan -- Rick Deckard -- Quinn Harris -- Han Solo

5. Stacee Jaxx -- Nick Morton -- Ray Ferrier -- Charlie Babbett -- Ethan Hunt

THE MOVIE LOVER'S CHALLENGE

The Real Name Game 3

Can you name the star from their birth name?

1. Krishna Pandit Bhanji

2. Katherine Matilda Swinton

3. Mark Sinclair

4. Demi Gene Guynes

5. Winona Laura Horowitz

6. Allan Stewart Konigsberg

7. Susan Alexandra Weaver

8. Margaret Mary Emily Anne Hyra

9. Ramón Antonio Gerardo Estévez

10. Michael John Douglas

THE MOVIE LOVER'S CHALLENGE

Movie Taglines 9

Challenge yourself to identify the films behind these iconic taglines.

1. He's got 14,000 eyewitnesses and no one saw a thing. (1998 - Thriller/ Crime)

2. The vacation is over. (1994 - Thriller/ Action)

3. Out here survival is everything. (2013 - Action/ Thriller)

4. Nothing Escapes Him. (2009 - Mystery/ Adventure)

5. Three Kids. One House. It's Alive! (2006 - Horror/ Comedy)

6. In the media circus of life, they were the main attraction. (1994 - Crime/ Action)

7. Life isn't measured in minutes, but in moments. (2008 - Romance/ Drama)

8. He's dying to become a chef. (2007 - Family/ Comedy)

9. Silently behind a door, it waits. (1991 - Drama/ Thriller)

10. You have a ringside seat for the bloodiest bicentennial in history! (1976 - Drama/ Sport)

THE MOVIE LOVER'S CHALLENGE

Many Names, Same Face 7

Identify the actor who portrayed all these characters.

1. Major Gwen Anderson -- Amanda Waller -- Nancy Birch -- Rose Maxson -- Ma Rainey

2. Steve Jobs -- Edwin Epps -- Lt. Archie Hicox -- Cal Lynch -- Erik Lehnsherr

3. Nolan Booth -- Guy -- Nmichael Bryce -- Hal Jordan -- Wade Wilson

4. Ron Woodroof -- Dallas -- Mark Hanna -- Steve Edison -- Buster Moon

5. Carol Vanstone -- Dr. Julia Harris -- Rose O'Reilly -- Grace Connelly -- Brooke Meyers

THE MOVIE LOVER'S CHALLENGE

Roles on Roles 15

Can you name the actor who has appeared in each set of movies?

1. Oblivion -- Possessor -- Roald Dahl's Matilda the Musical -- W.E.

2. Chappie -- District 9 -- Hardcore Henry -- The A-Team

3. Wind River -- Kodachrome -- Martha Marcy May Marlene -- Avengers: Infinity War

4. Central Intelligence -- Come and Find Me -- The Last House on the Left -- Need for Speed

5. Me and Earl and the Dying Girl -- Sound of Metal -- Thoroughbreds -- Ready Player One

THE MOVIE LOVER'S CHALLENGE

Movie Taglines 10

Challenge yourself to identify the films behind these iconic taglines.

1. This city is afraid of me. I've seen its true face. (2009 - Action/ Adventure)

2. A road trip that's going places... that aren't even on the map. (1998 - Comedy/ Adventure)

3. In the face of an enemy, in the heart of one man, lies the soul of a warrior. (2003 - Action/ War)

4. Stealin' stones and breakin' bones. (2000 - Crime/ Comedy)

5. Roll the dice and unleash the excitement! (1995 - Fantasy/ Adventure)

6. Protecting those who fear them. (2000 - Action/ Sci-fi)

7. Don't give away the ending - it's the only one we have! (1960 - Horror/ Thriller)

8. His father taught him to hate. His friends taught him rage. His enemies gave him hope. (1998 - Drama/ Crime)

9. Give yourself over to absolute pleasure. (1975 - Musical/ Horror)

10. Prepare to get served. (2009 - Family/ Comedy)

THE MOVIE LOVER'S CHALLENGE

Many Names, Same Face 8

Identify the actor who portrayed all these characters.

1. Charlie Kenton -- Bronson Peary -- Jean Valjean -- P.T. Barnum – Logan

2. John Cutter -- Hoagie Newcombe -- Alfie Elkins -- Alfred Pennyworth -- Charlie Croker

3. Ruby Thewes -- Anne Devereaux -- Dorothy Boyd -- Roxie Hart -- Bridget Jones

4. Dr. Michael Hfuhruhurr -- Dr Orin Scrivello D.D.S. -- Roger Cobb -- Lucky Day -- George Banks

5. Louis Bloom -- David Jordan -- Detective Loki -- Jack Twist -- Billy Hope

THE MOVIE LOVER'S CHALLENGE

Fantasy Flicks

1. In which fantasy film does a young girl named Sarah try to rescue her baby brother from the Goblin King?
2. In the movie "Maleficent," who plays the titular character Maleficent, a vengeful fairy who curses Princess Aurora?
3. Which fantasy film is based on the book by Cornelia Funke and follows the story of a young girl named Meggie and her father who can bring books to life?
4. Which movie involves a young boy named Bastian discovering a magical book that allows him to enter the world of Fantasia?
5. Which fantasy film features a protagonist named Westley and his quest to rescue Princess Buttercup?
6. In "Alice in Wonderland", what happens when Alice drinks the liquid labelled 'Drink Me'?
7. What is the name of the ancient wizard who guides and mentors the main character in "The Sorcerer's Apprentice"?
8. In "Harry Potter and the Chamber of Secrets", what Horcrux is destroyed when stabbed with the fang of a Basilisk?
9. Which 1985 fantasy film features Tom Cruise as a young man who must stop a demon lord from taking over the world?
10. What name did Gollum use in the Lord of the Rings movies before he became corrupted by the One Ring?

THE MOVIE LOVER'S CHALLENGE

THE MOVIE LOVER'S CHALLENGE

ANSWERS

THE MOVIE LOVER'S CHALLENGE

Role Recall 1 (Page 1)
1. Brad Pitt - Fight Club
2. Christian Bale - American Psycho
3. Vin Diesel - The Fast and The Furious
4. Al Pacino - Scarface
5. Kathy Bates - Misery
6. Jeremy Irons - The Lion King
7. Leonardo DiCaprio - Titanic
8. Mel Gibson - Braveheart
9. Kurt Russell - Guardians Of The Galaxy Volume 2
10. Vinnie Jones - Snatch

Age Is Just A Number 1 (Page 2)
1. Meryl Streep (1949)
   Tom Hanks (1956)
   Brad Pitt (1963)
   Julia Roberts (1967)
   Leonardo DiCaprio (1974)

2. Denzel Washington (1954)
   Johnny Depp (1963)
   Sandra Bullock (1964)
   Cate Blanchett (1969)
   Dwayne Johnson (1972)

3. Morgan Freeman (1937)
   Robert De Niro (1943)
   Nicole Kidman (1967)
   Will Smith (1968)
   Angelina Jolie (1975)

Can You Reel The Love Tonight? (Page 3)
1. Noah Calhoun

THE MOVIE LOVER'S CHALLENGE

2. Ghost
3. Pride & Prejudice
4. The Heart of the Ocean
5. What Women Want
6. Tom Hansen
7. The Proposal
8. Their names and personal information
9. Scarlett Johansson
10. Los Angeles

Roles on Roles 1 (Page 4)

1. Jeremy Renner
2. Elizabeth Banks
3. Aaron Eckhart
4. Anna Faris
5. John C. Reilly

Keeping It Vague 1 (Page 5)

1. The Silence Of The Lambs
2. Aladdin
3. Now You See Me

Roles on Roles 2 (Page 6)

1. Emile Hirsch
2. Judy Greer
3. Amanda Seyfried
4. Michael Peña
5. Christina Ricci

Complete The Title 1 (Page 7)

1. The Shape of Water
2. The Theory of Everything
3. Monty Python and the Holy Grail

THE MOVIE LOVER'S CHALLENGE

    4. Nocturnal Animals
    5. Crouching Tiger, Hidden Dragon
    6. Pulp Fiction
    7. Crazy Rich Asians
    8. Green Book
    9. My Fair Lady
    10. Gone with the Wind

Familiar Phrases 1 (Page 8)
    1. Star Wars: Episode IV - A New Hope
    2. Casablanca
    3. The Terminator
    4. The Dark Knight
    5. A Few Good Men
    6. The Wizard of Oz
    7. Titanic
    8. When Harry Met Sally...
    9. The Sixth Sense
    10. Forrest Gump

Release Date Challenge 1 (Page 9)
1. Goodfellas (1990)
   The Silence of the Lambs (1991)
   Schindler's List (1993)
   Pulp Fiction (1994)
   Titanic (1997)

2. Terminator 2: Judgment Day (1991)
   Jurassic Park (1993)
   The Shawshank Redemption (1994)
   Saving Private Ryan (1998)
   The Matrix (1999)

THE MOVIE LOVER'S CHALLENGE

3. Home Alone (1990)
   Forrest Gump (1994)
   Braveheart (1995)
   Fargo (1996)
   Fight Club (1999)

Movie Anagrams 1 (Page 10)
1. Psycho
2. Titanic
3. Rocky
4. The Godfather
5. Pulp Fiction
6. The Shawshank Redemption
7. The Silence of the Lambs
8. The Dark Knight
9. Inception
10. Interstellar

Role Recall 2 (Page 11)
1. John Cusack - Gross Pointe Blank
2. Audrey Hepburn - Breakfast at Tiffany's
3. Meryl Streep - The Devil Wears Prada
4. Jim Carrey - Dumb & Dumber
5. Jeff Goldblum - Jurassic Park
6. Kevin Spacey - American Beauty
7. Tom Hanks - Saving Mr Banks
8. John Travolta - Grease
9. Linda Hamilton - The Terminator
10. Jack Black - King Kong

Keeping It Vague 2 (Page 12)
1. The Matrix

2. Jurassic Park
3. E.T. The Extra-Terrestrial

Age Is Just A Number 2 (Page 13)
1.   George Clooney (1961)
   Matt Damon (1970)
   Kate Winslet (1975)
   Tom Hardy (1977)
   Natalie Portman (1981)

2.   Al Pacino (1940)
   Harrison Ford (1942)
   Samuel L. Jackson (1948)
   Christian Slater (1969)
   Benedict Cumberbatch (1976)

3.   Sean Connery (1930)
   Dustin Hoffman (1937)
   Liam Neeson (1952)
   Jennifer Aniston (1969)
   Emma Watson (1990)

Complete The Title 2 (Page 14)
1. 12 Angry Men
2. The Littlest Horse Thieves
3. Beauty and the Beast
4. Peter Pan
5. A Quiet Place
6. The Hobbit: The Desolation of Smaug
7. Fantastic Beasts and Where to Find Them
8. A Beautiful Mind
9. The Jungle Book
10. Hell or High Water

THE MOVIE LOVER'S CHALLENGE

Familiar Phrases 2 (Page 15)
1. Notting Hill
2. The Shining
3. Taxi Driver
4. The Godfather Part II
5. Top Gun
6. Pee-wee's Big Adventure
7. Apollo 13
8. Juno
9. Dr. No
10. Scarface

Release Date Challenge 2 (Page 16)
1. Speed (1994)
   Independence Day (1996)
   Men in Black (1997)
   The Truman Show (1998)
   The Sixth Sense (1999)

2. A Few Good Men (1992)
   Dumb and Dumber (1994)
   The Lord of the Rings: The Fellowship of the Ring (2001)
   The Dark Knight (2008)
   Avatar (2009)

3. Gladiator (2000)
   The Bourne Identity (2002)
   Finding Nemo (2003)
   The Departed (2006)
   Inception (2010)

THE MOVIE LOVER'S CHALLENGE

Roles on Roles 3 (Page 17)
    1. Chris Klein
    2. Mae Whitman
    3. Paul Dano
    4. Rosamund Pike
    5. Joel Kinnaman

Movie Anagrams 2 (Page 18)
    1. Forrest Gump
    2. Schindler's List
    3. Goodfellas
    4. The Matrix
    5. The Green Mile
    6. The Exorcist
    7. Snake Eyes
    8. Apocalypse Now
    9. One Flew Over the Cuckoo's Nest
    10. The French Connection

Role Recall 3 (Page 19)
    1. Jodie Foster - The Silence of the Lambs
    2. Anne Bancroft - The Graduate
    3. Joe Pesci - Goodfellas
    4. Morgan Freeman - The Shawshank Redemption
    5. Clint Eastwood - Dirty Harry
    6. Anthony Hopkins - The Silence of the Lambs
    7. Edward Furlong - Terminator 2: Judgment Day
    8. Mykelti Williamson - Forrest Gump
    9. Jesse Eisenberg - The Social Network
    10. Uma Thurman - Kill Bill Vol.1

Keeping It Vague 3 (Page 20)
    1. The Social Network

2. The Grand Budapest Hotel
3. La La Land

Age Is Just A Number 3 (Page 21)

1. Daniel Day-Lewis (1957)
   Tom Cruise (1962)
   Russell Crowe (1964)
   Gwyneth Paltrow (1972)
   Penelope Cruz (1974)

2. Robert Downey Jr (1965)
   Halle Berry (1966)
   Hugh Jackman (1968)
   Kate Hudson (1979)
   Keira Knightley (1985)

3. Clint Eastwood (1930)
   Jack Nicholson (1937)
   Jamie Foxx (1967)
   Cameron Diaz (1972)
   Amy Adams (1974)

Complete The Title 3 (Page 22)

1. The Hateful Eight
2. The Sound of Music
3. Reservoir Dogs
4. Moonrise Kingdom
5. The Social Network
6. The Grand Budapest Hotel
7. The Wolf of Wall Street
8. The Sixth Sense
9. Alice in Wonderland
10. Inside Out

THE MOVIE LOVER'S CHALLENGE

Familiar Phrases 3 (Page 23)
    1. Terminator 2: Judgment Day
    2. Toy Story
    3. The Silence of the Lambs
    4. Apocalypse Now
    5. The Devil Wears Prada
    6. A League of Their Own
    7. Jerry Maguire
    8. The Empire Strikes Back
    9. Midnight Cowboy
    10. Jerry Maguire

Release Date Challenge 3 (Page 24)

1. Memento (2000)
   Spider-Man (2002)
   Pirates of the Caribbean: The Curse of the Black Pearl (2003)
   The Notebook (2004)
   The Hangover (2009)

2. The Godfather (1972)
   Rocky (1976)
   Star Wars: Episode IV - A New Hope (1977)
   Raiders of the Lost Ark (1981)
   Blade Runner (1982)

3. Jaws (1975)
   The Terminator (1984)
   Back to the Future (1985)
   Dirty Dancing (1987)
   Die Hard (1988)

THE MOVIE LOVER'S CHALLENGE

Movie Anagrams 3 (Page 25)
    1. The Bridge on the River Kwai
    2. Vertigo
    3. The Graduate
    4. Amadeus
    5. Citizen Kane
    6. Casablanca
    7. Gone with the Wind
    8. Singin' in the Rain
    9. Some Like It Hot
    10. Lawrence of Arabia

Out of This World (Page 26)
    1. Replicants
    2. The OASIS
    3. Steven Spielberg
    4. Laurence Fishburne
    5. 88 miles per hour
    6. Guardians of the Galaxy
    7. Endurance
    8. Na'vi
    9. Jennifer Lawrence
    10. Jaegers

Roles on Roles 4 (Page 27)
    1. Brian Cox
    2. Joseph Gordon-Levitt
    3. Jena Malone
    4. Ethan Hawke
    5. Abbie Cornish

Role Recall 4 (Page 28)
    1. Matthew Broderick - The Cable Guy

THE MOVIE LOVER'S CHALLENGE

    2. Michael J Fox - Back To The Future
    3. Eddie Murphy - The Beverly Hills Cop
    4. Bill Murray - Ghostbusters
    5. Jeff Bridges - The Big Lebowski
    6. John Candy - Uncle Buck
    7. Laurence Fishburne - The Matrix
    8. Joaquin Phoenix - Joker
    9. Sigourney Weaver - Alien
    10. Johnny Depp - The Lone Ranger

Keeping It Vague 4 (Page 29)
    1. Avatar
    2. Jaws
    3. Fight Club

Age Is Just A Number 4 (Page 30)

1. Julianne Moore (1960)
   Jodie Foster (1962)
   Mark Wahlberg (1971)
   Reese Witherspoon (1976)
   Ryan Gosling (1980)

2. Colin Firth (1960)
   Eddie Murphy (1961)
   Charlize Theron (1975)
   Michael Fassbender (1977)
   Anne Hathaway (1982)

3. Matthew McConaughey (1969)
   Christian Bale (1974)
   Marion Cotillard (1975)
   Rachel McAdams (1978)
   Jennifer Lawrence (1990)

THE MOVIE LOVER'S CHALLENGE

Complete The Title 4 (Page 31)
1. Rogue One: A Star Wars Story
2. The Green Mile
3. Lady and the Tramp
4. Blue is the Warmest Color
5. The Ballad of Buster Scruggs
6. Django Unchained
7. The Truman Show
8. The Black Stallion
9. American Beauty
10. Marriage Story

Familiar Phrases 4 (Page 32)
1. Who Framed Roger Rabbit?
2. The Lord of the Rings: The Fellowship of the Ring
3. There Will Be Blood
4. Forrest Gump
5. The Big Lebowski
6. Captain America: The First Avenger
7. My Girl
8. Titanic
9. Die Hard
10. The Godfather

Release Date Challenge 4 (Page 33)
1. Casablanca (1942)
   The Sound of Music (1965)
   The Exorcist (1973)
   The Social Network (2010)
   La La Land (2016)

THE MOVIE LOVER'S CHALLENGE

2.   The King's Speech (2010)
           The Dark Knight Rises (2012)
           The Grand Budapest Hotel (2014)
           The Shape of Water (2017)
           Black Panther (2018)

3.   The Graduate (1967)
           Easy Rider (1969)
           The French Connection (1971)
           The Sting (1973)
           One Flew Over the Cuckoo's Nest (1975)

Movie Anagrams 4 (Page 34)
1. The Sound of Music
2. Midnight Cowboy
3. A Clockwork Orange
4. Dog Day Afternoon
5. Network
6. Annie Hall
7. Rain Man
8. Good Will Hunting
9. American Beauty
10. Gladiator

Role Recall 5 (Page 35)
1. Steve Martin - Father of the Bride
2. Denzel Washington - Training Day
3. Tim Curry - The Rocky Horror Picture Show
4. Jack Black - School Of Rock
5. Bruce Willis - The Sixth Sense
6. Courteney Cox - Scream
7. Leonardo DiCaprio - Inception
8. Samuel L Jackson - Pulp Fiction

9. Steve Buscemi - Reservoir Dogs
10. Sarah Jessica Parker - Sex and the City

Keeping It Vague 5 (Page 36)
1. Point Break
2. Back to the Future
3. Rocky

Roles on Roles 5 (Page 37)
1. Jay Baruchel
2. Lena Headey
3. Paul Rudd
4. Zooey Deschanel
5. Ryan Phillippe

Complete The Title 5 (Page 38)
1. Apocalypse Now
2. Hacksaw Ridge
3. Knives Out
4. The Big Short
5. Lost in Translation
6. Full Metal Jacket
7. The Great Escape
8. The Bridge on the River Kwai
9. Baby Driver
10. Oliver & Company

Age Is Just A Number 5 (Page 39)
1. Michelle Pfeiffer (1958)
   Ben Affleck (1972)
   Ryan Reynolds (1976)
   Eddie Redmayne (1982)
   Brie Larson (1989)

THE MOVIE LOVER'S CHALLENGE

2.   Viola Davis (1965)
   Octavia Spencer (1970)
   Chadwick Boseman (1976)
   Chris Pratt (1979)
   Margot Robbie (1990)

3.   Mahershala Ali (1974)
   Jason Momoa (1979)
   Lupita Nyong'o (1983)
   Gal Gadot (1985)
   Emma Stone (1988)

Familiar Phrases 5 (Page 40)
1. The Karate Kid
2. Some Like It Hot
3. V for Vendetta
4. Back to The Future
5. Tombstone
6. Airplane!
7. Armageddon
8. Waterworld
9. Independence Day
10. Starship Troopers

Release Date Challenge 5 (Page 41)
1.   A Clockwork Orange (1971)
   The Rocky Horror Picture Show (1975)
   Taxi Driver (1976)
   Close Encounters of the Third Kind (1977)
   Alien (1979)

2.   Spirited Away (2001)
   Lost in Translation (2003)

THE MOVIE LOVER'S CHALLENGE

       The Aviator (2004)
       No Country for Old Men (2007)
       Up (2009)

3.   The Hurt Locker (2008)
       Black Swan (2010)
       Mad Max: Fury Road (2015)
       Arrival (2016)
       Get Out (2017)

Movie Anagrams 5 (Page 42)
1. The Royal Tenenbaums
2. Lost in Translation
3. The Social Network
4. Get Out
5. Parasite
6. The Maltese Falcon
7. Double Indemnity
8. On the Waterfront
9. Rebel Without a Cause
10. Breakfast at Tiffany's

Role Recall 6 (Page 43)
1. Christian Slater - Robin Hood: Prince of Thieves
2. Tom Hanks - Saving Private Ryan
3. Michael Caine - Batman Begins
4. Frances McDormand - Fargo
5. Edward Norton - American History X
6. Robert Downey Jr - Iron Man
7. Danny DeVito - Twins
8. Robert De Niro - Taxi Driver
9. Bruce Willis - Die Hard
10. Meg Ryan - When Harry Met Sally

THE MOVIE LOVER'S CHALLENGE

Keeping It Vague 6 (Page 44)
    1. The Exorcist
    2. A Clockwork Orange
    3. The Deer Hunter

Age Is Just A Number 6 (Page 45)

1. Sylvester Stallone (1946)
   Arnold Schwarzenegger (1947)
   Idris Elba (1972)
   Joaquin Phoenix (1974)
   Tessa Thompson (1983)

2. Mel Gibson (1956)
   Carey Elwes (1962)
   Rami Malek (1981)
   Adam Driver (1983)
   Florence Pugh (1996)

3. Neve Campbell (1973)
   Oscar Isaac (1979)
   Chris Evans (1981)
   Chris Hemsworth (1983)
   John Boyega (1992)

Roles on Roles 6 (Page 46)
    1. Rachel Bilson
    2. James Marsden
    3. Brittany Murphy
    4. Cillian Murphy
    5. Bruce Willis

THE MOVIE LOVER'S CHALLENGE

Complete The Title 6 (Page 47)
1. Isle of Dogs
2. A Clockwork Orange
3. Lawrence of Arabia
4. The King's Speech
5. Inglourious Basterds
6. The Day the Earth Stood Still
7. Doctor Strange
8. First Reformed
9. Black Panther
10. Once Upon a Time in Hollywood

Familiar Phrases 6 (Page 48)
1. Robocop
2. Gone with the Wind
3. Dirty Harry
4. Animal Crackers
5. On the Waterfront
6. The Wizard of Oz
7. Psycho
8. Wall Street
9. Sunset Boulevard
10. All About Eve

Release Date Challenge 6 (Page 49)

1. Amélie (2001)
   Children of Men (2006)
   Once (2007)
   A Separation (2011)
   The Revenant (2015)

2. The Royal Tenenbaums (2001)
   There Will Be Blood (2007)

THE MOVIE LOVER'S CHALLENGE

    Inglourious Basterds (2009)
    The Artist (2011)
    Inside Out (2015)

3.   Crouching Tiger, Hidden Dragon (2000)
    Donnie Darko (2001)
    City of God (2002)
    Kill Bill: Vol 1 (2003)
    The Tree of Life (2011)

Movie Anagrams 6 (Page 50)
1. To Kill a Mockingbird
2. Bonnie and Clyde
3. Rosemary's Baby
4. The Sting
5. The Deer Hunter
6. Alien
7. Blade Runner
8. The Elephant Man
9. Gandhi
10. The Killing Fields

The Drama Diaries (Page 51)
1. Andy Dufresne
2. Steven Spielberg
3. Persepolis
4. John Malkovich
5. Whiplash
6. Equilibrium
7. John Nash
8. The Danish Girl
9. Barry Jenkins
10. Black Swan

THE MOVIE LOVER'S CHALLENGE

Roles on Roles 7 (Page 52)
1. Adam Scott
2. Maggie Gyllenhaal
3. Emilia Clarke
4. Sam Rockwell
5. Jordana Brewster

Role Recall 7 (Page 53)
1. Harrison Ford - The Fugitive
2. Kate Winslet - Titanic
3. Cameron Diaz - Charlie's Angels
4. Bruce Willis - The Fifth Element
5. Keanu Reeves - Point Break
6. Gregory Peck - To Kill a Mockingbird
7. Matthew Broderick - Godzilla
8. Anthony Perkins - Psycho
9. Kurt Russell - Big Trouble In Little China
10. Zoe Saldana - Avatar

Keeping It Vague 7 (Page 54)
1. Schindler's List
2. Goodfellas
3. Dances With Wolves

Complete The Title 7 (Page 55)
1. If Beale Street Could Talk
2. Jojo Rabbit
3. Doctor Zhivago
4. Dead Poets Society
5. Good Will Hunting
6. Hidden Figures
7. The Imitation Game

THE MOVIE LOVER'S CHALLENGE

    8. Mad Max: Fury Road
    9. Black Swan
    10. Shutter Island

Familiar Phrases 7 (Page 56)
    1. Cool Hand Luke
    2. Love Story
    3. The Maltese Falcon
    4. In the Heat of the Night
    5. Citizen Kane
    6. White Heat
    7. Network
    8. Casablanca
    9. The Silence of the Lambs
    10. Sunset Boulevard

Release Date Challenge 7 (Page 57)

1. Annie Hall (1977)
   Apocalypse Now (1979)
   Beverly Hills Cop (1984)
   The Breakfast Club (1985)
   The Green Mile (1999)

2. The Shining (1980)
   E.T. the Extra-Terrestrial (1982)
   Platoon (1986)
   Toy Story (1995)
   American Beauty (1999)

3. Forrest Gump (1994)
   Downfall (2004)
   Whiplash (2014)
   The Farewell (2019)

THE MOVIE LOVER'S CHALLENGE

Shang-Chi and the Legend of the Ten Rings (2021)

Movie Anagrams 7 (Page 58)

    1. Platoon
    2. Dead Poets Society
    3. Unforgiven
    4. The English Patient
    5. Fargo
    6. The Big Lebowski
    7. Almost Famous
    8. The Third Man
    9. Rear Window
    10. West Side Story

Lights, Camera, Laughter! (Page 59)

    1. Liar Liar
    2. Bill & Ted's Excellent Adventure
    3. Trading Places
    4. Seth and Evan
    5. Las Vegas
    6. I Got You Babe by Sonny & Cher
    7. Sister Act
    8. Hot Fuzz
    9. A dance routine
    10. Harry and Marv

Same Name, Different Faces 1 (Page 60)

    1. Alfred Pennyworth
    2. James Bond
    3. Hannibal Lecter
    4. Clark Kent/ Superman
    5. Sherlock Holmes
    6. Peter Parker/ Spiderman

THE MOVIE LOVER'S CHALLENGE

    7. Dracula
    8. Selina Kyle/ Catwoman
    9. Inspector Clouseau
    10. Robin Hood

Role Recall 8 (Page 61)

    1. George Clooney - Ocean's Eleven
    2. Bruce Willis - Armageddon
    3. Robert Englund - A Nightmare on Elm Street
    4. Leonardo DiCaprio - Gangs of New York
    5. Carrie-Anne Moss - The Matrix
    6. Christoph Waltz - Inglourious Basterds
    7. Natalie Portman - Black Swan
    8. Marlon Brando - The Godfather
    9. Aaron Eckhart - The Dark Knight
    10. John Goodman - The Big Lebowski

Keeping It Vague 8 (Page 62)

    1. Pitch Perfect
    2. The Breakfast Club
    3. 40 Year Old Virgin

Roles on Roles 8 (Page 63)

    1. Jack Huston
    2. Alice Eve
    3. Charlie Cox
    4. Mary Elizabeth Winstead
    5. Jesse Eisenberg

Complete The Title 8 (Page 64)

    1. Manchester by the Sea
    2. Finding Nemo
    3. Snow White and the Seven Dwarfs

THE MOVIE LOVER'S CHALLENGE

    4. Uncut Gems
    5. The Guns of Navarone
    6. Blade Runner 2049
    7. The Usual Suspects
    8. Ex Machina
    9. Dallas Buyers Club
    10. Sleeping Beauty

Familiar Phrases 8 (Page 65)

    1. She Done Him Wrong
    2. Grand Hotel
    3. Gone with the Wind
    4. Casablanca
    5. Field of Dreams
    6. Planet of the Apes
    7. Poltergeist
    8. Marathon Man
    9. 2001: A Space Odyssey
    10. National Lampoon's Animal House

Release Date Challenge 8 (Page 66)

1.   Heat (1995)
    Skyfall (2012)
    The Gift (2015)
    Toy Story 4 (2019)
    Minari (2020)

2.   Batman Returns (1992)
    The Lion King (1994)
    Catch Me If You Can (2002)
    The Salesman (2016)
    Good Time (2017)

3.   Princess Mononoke (1997)

THE MOVIE LOVER'S CHALLENGE

> Fear and Loathing in Las Vegas (1998)
> Birdman (2014)
> One Night in Miami (2020)
> The Tragedy of Macbeth (2021)

Movie Anagrams 8 (Page 67)
1. Butch Cassidy and the Sundance Kid
2. The Last Picture Show
3. Deliverance
4. Chinatown
5. Nashville
6. Raging Bull
7. Das Boot
8. Tootsie
9. The Color Purple
10. Blue Velvet

Role Recall 9 (Page 68)
1. Kevin Spacey - The Usual Suspects
2. Jack Nicholson - One Flew Over The Cuckoo's Nest
3. Jennifer Lawrence - The Hunger Games
4. Tom Cruise - Mission: Impossible
5. Tim Robbins - The Shawshank Redemption
6. Anjelica Houston - The Addams Family
7. Humphrey Bogart - Casablanca
8. Macauley Culkin - Home Alone
9. Wesley Snipes - Demolition Man
10. Jamie Dornan - Fifty Shades of Grey

Dogs on Film (Page 69)
1. Milo
2. Baxter
3. Saint Bernard

4. Fifteen
5. Bolt
6. Isle of Dogs
7. French Mastiff
8. Toto
9. Dante
10. Max

Keeping It Vague 9 (Page 70)
1. Psycho
2. The Martian
3. Apocalypse Now

Family Film Frenzy (Page 71)
1. Syndrome
2. Coraline
3. Gertie
4. National Institute of Mental Health
5. A hornbill
6. Geppetto
7. Hogarth Hughes
8. Tuppence (Two pence)
9. The Dark Crystal
10. The Electromagnetic Shrinking Machine

Complete The Title 9 (Page 72)
1. Call Me By Your Name
2. The Lion King
3. Straight Outta Compton
4. A Star is Born
5. Little Women
6. Train to Busan
7. Bohemian Rhapsody

THE MOVIE LOVER'S CHALLENGE

    8. Phantom Thread
    9. Eighth Grade
    10. Sorry to Bother You

Familiar Phrases 9 (Page 73)
    1. The Lord of the Rings: The Two Towers
    2. Dirty Dancing
    3. Terminator 2: Judgment Day
    4. Mean Girls
    5. Blade Runner
    6. Bridget Jones's Diary
    7. The Devil Wears Prada
    8. It's A Wondeful Life
    9. Babe
    10. Ferris Bueller's Day Off

Release Date Challenge 9 (Page 74)

1. The Sting (1973)
   Gremlins (1984)
   The 'Burbs (1989)
   The X-Files (1998)
   The Hunt for the Wilderpeople (2016)

2. The Untouchables (1987)
   The Incredibles (2004)
   Hostel (2005)
   Watchmen (2009)
   The Other Guys (2010)

3. The Princess Bride (1987)
   Batman Begins (2005)
   Blade Runner 2049 (2017)
   A Star Is Born (2018)

THE MOVIE LOVER'S CHALLENGE

No Time to Die (2021)

Movie Anagrams 9 (Page 75)
1. Guardians Of The Galaxy
2. The Italian Job
3. Doctor Sleep
4. A Room With A View
5. Nightcrawler
6. The Dam Busters
7. Dumb and Dumber
8. Day of the Dead
9. The Prestige
10. Police Academy

Same Name, Different Faces 2 (Page 76)
1. Gellert Grindelwald
2. Bruce Wayne/ Batman
3. Robin Hood
4. Elizabeth Bennet
5. Hercule Poirot
6. Cinderella
7. Tarzan
8. Jack Ryan
9. Steve Rogers/ Captain America
10. Bruce Banner/ The Hulk

Role Recall 10 (Page 77)
1. Jim Carrey - The Mask
2. Will Smith - Independence Day
3. Rick Moranis - Honey, I Shrunk The Kids
4. Sandra Bullock - Miss Congeniality
5. Naomi Watts - King Kong
6. Arnold Schwarzenegger - Last Action Hero

THE MOVIE LOVER'S CHALLENGE

    7. Vivien Leigh - Gone With The Wind
    8. Christoph Waltz - Django Unchained
    9. Reese Witherspoon - Legally Blonde
    10. Judy Garland - The Wizard of Oz

Keeping It Vague 10 (Page 78)
    1. Do The Right Thing
    2. White Men Can't Jump
    3. Edward Scissorhands

Complete The Title 10 (Page 79)
    1. Winter's Bone
    2. Roman Holiday
    3. Robin Hood
    4. Eternal Sunshine of the Spotless Mind
    5. Jurassic Park
    6. Invasion of the Body Snatchers
    7. The Disaster Artist
    8. Breakfast at Tiffany's
    9. Gone Girl
    10. The Big Lebowski

Roles on Roles 9 (Page 80)
    1. Freida Pinto
    2. Topher Grace
    3. Rashida Jones
    4. Jason Schwartzman
    5. Emily Mortimer

Familiar Phrases 10 (Page 81)
    1. Black Panther
    2. The Shawshank Redemption
    3. The Hangover Part II

4. The Princess Bride
5. Se7en
6. The Dark Knight
7. Hook
8. Dead Poets Society
9. Gladiator
10. Avengers: Endgame

Release Date Challenge 10 (Page 82)

1. Easy Rider (1969)
   Wedding Crashers (2005)
   Frozen (2013)
   Edge of Tomorrow (2014)
   Black Mass (2015)

2. Trading Places (1983)
   Labyrinth (1986)
   Enemy of The State (1998)
   Cloudy with a Chance of Meatballs (2009)
   Captain America: The First Avenger (2011)

3. Swiss Army Man (2016)
   When Harry Met Sally (1989)
   The Notebook (2004)
   The Revenant (2015)
   Alita: Battle Angel (2019)

Movie Anagrams 10 (Page 83)

1. The Rocky Horror Picture Show
2. Unbreakable
3. The Great Outdoors
4. Cloudy With A Chance Of Meatballs
5. Legally Blonde

THE MOVIE LOVER'S CHALLENGE

    6. Drop Dead Fred
    7. Edward Scissorhands
    8. Letters From Iwo Jima
    9. Stuck On You
    10. Halloween

Movie Villains (Page 84)
    1. One Flew Over the Cuckoo's Nest
    2. Misery
    3. Die Hard
    4. The Texas Chainsaw Massacre
    5. American Psycho
    6. Fatal Attraction
    7. The Deviil Wears Prada
    8. From Russia with Love
    9. A Clockwork Orange
    10. Taxi Driver

Roles on Roles 10 (Page 85)
    1. Michael Sheen
    2. Dan Stevens
    3. Chloe Grace Moretz
    4. James Franco
    5. Evan Rachel Wood

Famous Voices 1 (Page 86)
    1. Batty Koda
    2. Oscar
    3. Lightning McQueen
    4. James P Sullivan
    5. Mrs. Potts
    6. Hades
    7. Barry B. Benson

THE MOVIE LOVER'S CHALLENGE

8. Mushu
9. Lord Farquaad
10. Scar

Direct Orders 1 (Page 87)

1. Aliens (1986)
   The Abyss (1989)
   Terminator 2: Judgment Day (1991)
   Titanic (1997)
   Avatar (2009)

2. Alien (1979)
   Blade Runner (1982)
   Gladiator (2000)
   Black Hawk Down (2001)
   The Martian (2015)

3. Jaws (1975)
   Raiders Of The Lost Ark (1981)
   E.T. the Extra-Terrestrial (1982)
   Jurassic Park (1993)
   Saving Private Ryan (1998)

4. Memento (2000)
   The Dark Knight (2008)
   Inception (2010)
   Interstellar (2014)
   Dunkirk (2017)

Famous Voices 2 (Page 88)

1. Buzz Lightyear
2. Oh
3. Weaver

THE MOVIE LOVER'S CHALLENGE

4. Francis
5. Queen Tara
6. John Smith
7. Stinky Pete
8. Emmet Brickowski
9. Flint Lockwood
10. Metro Man

Roles on Roles 11 (Page 89)

1. Christina Applegate
2. Ethan Embry
3. Gugu Mbatha-Raw
4. Josh Lucas
5. Bryce Dallas Howard

Direct Orders 2 (Page 90)

1. 2001: A Space Odyssey (1968)
   A Clockwork Orange (1971)
   Barry Lyndon (1975)
   The Shining (1980)
   Full Metal Jacket (1987)

2. Rear Window (1954)
   Vertigo (1958)
   North By Northwest (1959)
   Psycho (1960)
   The Birds (1963)

3. Taxi Driver (1976)
   Raging Bull (1980)
   Goodfellas (1990)
   Casino (1995)
   The Departed (2006)

4.   Reservoir Dogs (1992)
     Pulp Fiction (1994)
     Kill Bill: Volume 1 (2003)
     Inglorious Basterds (2009)
     Django Unchained (2012)

Blockbuster Brawls (Page 91)
1. Nakatomi Plaza
2. Keanu Reeves
3. Raoul Silva
4. The Bride
5. George Miller
6. Mega-City One
7. Ethan Hunt
8. Rampage
9. Joaquin Phoenix
10. Quentin Tarantino

Famous Voices 3 (Page 92)
1. Mr Incredible/ Bob Parr
2. Lance Sterling
3. Ian Lightfoot
4. Butch
5. Chick Hicks
6. Colonel Cutter
7. Buck Wild
8. Stoick
9. Joy
10. Olaf

Direct Orders 3 (Page 93)

THE MOVIE LOVER'S CHALLENGE

1. Patton (1970)
   The Godfather (1972)
   The Conversation (1974)
   Apocalypse Now (1979)
   Runble Fish (1983)

2. Rashoman (1950)
   Seven Samurai (1954)
   Throne Of Blood (1957)
   Yojimbo (1961)
   Ran (1985)

3. Se7en (1995)
   Fight Club (1999)
   Zodiac (2007)
   The Social Network (2010)
   Gone Girl (2014)

4. Rushmorre (1998)
   The Royal Tenenbaums (2001)
   Fantastic Mr. Fox (2009)
   Moonrise Kingdom (2012)
   The Grand Budapest Hotel (2014)

Roles on Roles 12 (Page 94)
1. Luke Evans
2. Michelle Monaghan
3. Sam Worthington
4. Lucy Liu
5. Robert De Niro

Movie Taglines 1 (Page 95)

THE MOVIE LOVER'S CHALLENGE

1. Alien
2. Superman
3. The Shawshank Redemption
4. Forrest Gump
5. Highlander
6. The Fly
7. Back to the Future Part II
8. A Few Good Men
9. Poltergeist
10. Jaws

Direct Orders 4 (Page 96)

1. Unforgiven (1992)
   Mystic River (2003)
   Million Dollar Baby (2004)
   Flags Of Our Fathers (2006)
   Gran Torino (2008)

2. Hellboy (2004)
   Pan's Labyrinth (2006)
   Pacific Rim (2013)
   Crimson Peak (2015)
   The Shape Of Water (2017)

3. Beetlejuice (1988)
   Batman (1989)
   Edward Scissorhands (1990)
   Big Fish (2003)
   Corpse Bride (2005)

4. The Virgin Suicides (1999)
   Lost In Translation (2003)
   Marie Antionette (2006)

Somewhere (2010)
The Bling Ring (2013)

Movie Taglines 2 (Page 97)
1. Indiana Jones and the Temple of Doom
2. The Lord of the Rings: The Fellowship of the Ring
3. 300
4. Blade Runner
5. Finding Nemo
6. Jurassic Park
7. Apollo 13
8. Monty Python's Life of Brian
9. Ghostbusters
10. Serenity

Direct Orders 5 (Page 98)

1. Citizen Kane (1941)
   The Magnificent Andersons (1942)
   The Lady From Shanghai (1947)
   Touch Of Evil (1958)
   Chimes Of Midnight (1965)

2. Do The Right Thing (1989)
   Jungle Fever (1991)
   Malcolm X (1992)
   25th Hour (2002)
   BlacKkKlansman (2018)

3. Sense and Sensibility (1995)
   Crouching Tiger, Hidden Dragon (2000)
   Brokeback Mountain (2005)
   Lust, Caution (2007)
   Life Of Pi (2012)

4. Near Dark (1987)
Point Break (1991)
The Hurt Locker (2008)
Zero Dark Thirty (2012)
Detroit (2017)

Movie Taglines 3 (Page 99)
1. Armageddon
2. Edward Scissorhands
3. Now You See Me
4. Chicken Run
5. The Bourne Identity
6. Iron Man
7. Star Wars: Episode IV - A New Hope
8. Schindler's List
9. Divergent
10. The X-Files

Many Names, Same Face 1 (Page 100)
1. Gary Sinise
2. Meryl Streep
3. John Heard
4. John Travolta
5. Daniel Day-Lewis

Movie Taglines 4 (Page 101)
1. Braveheart
2. Interstellar
3. GoldenEye
4. Mission: Impossible III
5. Batman Begins
6. The Matrix

7. Inception
8. Fargo
9. Con Air
10. The Naked Gun: From the Files of Police Squad!

Many Names, Same Face 2 (Page 102)
1. Sylvester Stallone
2. Leonardo DiCaprio
3. Jennifer Lawrence
4. Nicolas Cage
5. Jack Nicholson

Roles on Roles 13 (Page 103)
1. Alice Braga
2. Timothy Olyphant
3. Carla Gugino
4. Scott Speedman
5. Sarah Paulson

Fright Night Flicks (Page 104)
1. Michael Myers
2. The Evil Dead
3. Pazuzu
4. The Overlook Hotel
5. The Ring
6. Freddy Krueger
7. The Conjuring
8. Mia Farrow
9. The Thing
10. Pinhead

Movie Taglines 5 (Page 105)

THE MOVIE LOVER'S CHALLENGE

1. Mr. Nobody
2. Scott Pilgrim vs. the World
3. American Pie
4. Get Out
5. Saving Private Ryan
6. Robin Hood
7. The Notebook
8. Saw
9. The Best Exotic Marigold Hotel
10. In Bruges

Many Names, Same Face 3 (Page 106)
1. Arnold Schwarzenegger
2. Jim Carrey
3. Robert De Niro
4. Tom Hanks
5. Denzel Washington

Movie Taglines 6 (Page 107)
1. Cool Runnings
2. Finding Dory
3. Captain America: The First Avenger
4. 1917
5. Sonic the Hedgehog
6. Mary Poppins Returns
7. The Insider
8. The First Wives Club
9. The NeverEnding Story
10. Judge Dredd

The Real Name Game 1 (Page 108)
1. Tom Cruise
2. Meryl Streep

THE MOVIE LOVER'S CHALLENGE

3. Emma Stone
4. Natalie Portman
5. Whoopi Goldberg
6. Jamie Foxx
7. Joaquin Phoenix
8. Nicolas Cage
9. Brad Pitt
10. Marilyn Monroe

Many Names, Same Face 4 (Page 109)

1. Charlize Theron
2. Brad Pitt
3. Angelina Jolie
4. Johnny Depp
5. Al Pacino

Movie Taglines 7 (Page 110)

1. Turner & Hooch
2. Ferris Bueller's Day Off
3. Rough Night
4. Cobra
5. Hercules
6. Collateral
7. The Wizard of Oz
8. The Muppets
9. Bedknobs and Broomsticks
10. Parasite

Roles on Roles 14 (Page 111)

1. Tom Hardy
2. Camilla Belle
3. David Oyelowo
4. Alison Brie

THE MOVIE LOVER'S CHALLENGE

5. Dominic Cooper

The Real Name Game 2 (Page 112)
1. Miley Cyrus
2. Michael Caine
3. Tom Hardy
4. John Boyega
5. Jodie Foster
6. Brie Larson
7. Helen Mirren
8. Diane Keaton
9. Julianne Moore
10. Christopher Walken

True Stories (Page 113)
1. Julia Roberts
2. Dallas Buyers Club
3. David Fincher
4. Cool Runnings
5. The Pursuit of Happyness
6. Leonardo DiCaprio
7. American football
8. Professor Stephen Hawking
9. N.A.S.A.
10. Raging Bull

Many Names, Same Face 5 (Page 114)
1. Cate Blanchett
2. Morgan Freeman
3. Emma Stone
4. Natalie Portman
5. Will Smith

THE MOVIE LOVER'S CHALLENGE

Movie Taglines 8 (Page 115)
    1. True Lies
    2. Gladiator
    3. The Incredibles
    4. Titanic
    5. The Hobbit: The Desolation of Smaug
    6. Toy Story 4
    7. Brokeback Mountain
    8. The Terminator
    9. La La Land
    10. Catch Me If You Can

Many Names, Same Face 6 (Page 116)
    1. Julia Roberts
    2. Scarlett Johansson
    3. Chris Pratt
    4. Harrison Ford
    5. Tom Cruise

The Real Name Game 3 (Page 117)
    1. Ben Kingsley
    2. Tilda Swinton
    3. Vin Diesel
    4. Demi Moore
    5. Winona Ryder
    6. Woody Allen
    7. Sigourney Weaver
    8. Meg Ryan
    9. Martin Sheen
    10. Michael Keaton

Movie Taglines 9 (Page 118)

THE MOVIE LOVER'S CHALLENGE

1. Snake Eyes
2. The River Wild
3. Captain Phillips
4. Sherlock Holmes
5. Monster House
6. Natural Born Killers
7. The Curious Case of Benjamin Button
8. Ratatouille
9. Backdraft
10. Rocky

Many Names, Same Face 7 (Page 119)

1. Viola Davis
2. Michael Fassbender
3. Ryan Reynolds
4. Matthew McConaughey
5. Jennifer Aniston

Roles on Roles 15 (Page 120)

1. Andrea Riseborough
2. Sharlto Copley
3. Elizabeth Olsen
4. Aaron Paul
5. Olivia Cooke

Movie Taglines 10 (Page 121)

1. Watchmen
2. Fear and Loathing in Las Vegas
3. The Last Samurai
4. Snatch
5. Jumanji
6. X-Men
7. Psycho

THE MOVIE LOVER'S CHALLENGE

    8. American History X
    9. The Rocky Horror Picture Show
    10. Cloudy with a Chance of Meatballs

Many Names, Same Face 8 (Page 122)
    1. Hugh Jackman
    2. Michael Caine
    3. Renée Zellweger
    4. Steve Martin
    5. Jake Gyllenhaal

Fantasy Flicks (Page 123)
    1. Labyrinth
    2. Angelina Jolie
    3. Inkheart
    4. The NeverEnding Story
    5. The Princess Bride
    6. She shrinks
    7. Balthazar Blake
    8. Tom Riddle's Diary
    9. Legend
    10. Sméagol

Printed in Dunstable, United Kingdom